P9-CRD-307

~~EXTRA~~ORDINARY

HOW TO ~~CONQUER~~ turn THE WORLD upside down

TONY MERIDA

LifeWay Press®
Nashville, Tennessee

Published by LifeWay Press® · © 2014 Tony Merida · Reprinted 2016

No part of this work may be reproduced or transmitted in any form or by any means, electronic or mechanical, including photocopying and recording, or by any information storage or retrieval system, except as may be expressly permitted in writing by the publisher. Requests for permission should be addressed in writing to LifeWay Press®; One LifeWay Plaza; Nashville, TN 37234-0152.

ISBN 978-1-4300-3220-5 8 · Item 005644104

Dewey decimal classification: 248.84
Subject headings: CHRISTIAN LIFE \ MINISTRY \ SOCIAL JUSTICE

Unless otherwise noted all Scripture quotations are taken from the Holman Christian Standard Bible®, © copyright 1999, 2000, 2002, 2003 by Holman Bible Publishers. Used by permission. Scripture quotations marked CEV are taken from the Contemporary English Version. Copyright © 1991, 1992, 1995 by American Bible Society. Used by permission. Scripture quotations marked ESV are taken from The Holy Bible, English Standard Version® (ESV®), copyright © 2001 by Crossway, a publishing ministry of Good News Publishers. Used by permission. All rights reserved. Scripture quotations marked NASB are taken from the New American Standard Bible®, Copyright © 1960, 1962, 1963, 1968, 1971, 1972, 1973, 1975, 1977, 1995 by The Lockman Foundation. Used by permission. (lockman.org)

To order additional copies of this resource, write to LifeWay Resources Customer Service; One LifeWay Plaza; Nashville, TN 37234-0113; fax 615.251.5933; phone toll free 800.458.2772; order online at lifeway.com; email orderentry@lifeway.com; or visit the LifeWay Christian Store serving you.

Printed in the United States of America

Groups Ministry Publishing · LifeWay Resources
One LifeWay Plaza · Nashville, TN 37234-0152

TABLE OF CONTENTS

HOW TO USE THIS STUDY

Each session will contain the following format:

OPEN: Begin your time by watching a teaching video led by Tony that will introduce the topic for each session. Watching this together and taking notes will enrich your discussion and may provide additional insight into the session's discussion questions.

You'll then transition into the group time with icebreakers, further introducing the topic you'll be discussing over the next week.

DISCUSS AND APPLY: These times are designed to build on the lessons taught in the video by looking at additional passages of Scripture and applying them to your own life situation. This works best when you work through the questions individually before gathering together.

Come into the discussion ready to share what God showed you in your own study. If you're stumped on a question, you can look forward to asking for insight from group members during your time together.

ACTION: For each group time we've provided more practical steps to help your group encourage one another to put into action what you've learned from God's Word. These pages along with the individual-study portion provide an opportunity to solidify your move toward living a life of everyday, ordinary justice.

This section will also give you a more detailed look into the individual study to come and a prayer guide as you close your time together.

INDIVIDUAL STUDY: More in-depth study for each session is provided for your personal study time. Take time to read and interact with this section as you meet with God for the first few days following your group time. The topics will address concepts you've just studied with your group, encouraging you to read additional Scripture passages and answer some questions. The Moving Toward Action section will solidify your action steps toward justice.

ABOUT THE AUTHOR

Tony Merida is the founding pastor of Imago Dei Church in Raleigh, North Carolina. He also serves as an associate professor of preaching at Southeastern Baptist Theological Seminary. Tony and his wife, Kimberly, have five adopted children: Angela, Jana, Victoria, James, and Joshua.

Tony has quickly become a leading voice in the growing movement for adoption and orphan care. His passion for the fatherless is evident through his writing, teaching, and speaking. Tony speaks around the world at a variety of events, including church-planting conferences, pastors conferences, orphan-care events, student camps, and courses at theological institutions.

Tony is the author of *Ordinary* and *Faithful Preaching* and a coauthor of *Orphanology*. Also, along with David Platt and Danny Akin, Tony serves as a general editor of and contributor to a commentary series with B&H Publishing Group titled *Christ-Centered Exposition*.

Find out more about Tony online at *tonymerida.net*.

EVERYDAY JUSTICE

TRADING SENSATIONALISM
FOR ORDINARY CHRISTIANITY

View video session 1 as a group and then dive into the discussion guide below.

OPEN

If this is your first experience as a small-group community, take time for brief introductions. As an icebreaker, consider sharing how each member came to be a part of your group.

Defining Christianity is different from defining a Christian. One depicts a movement. The other describes a person. Engage the following activity as a group. First, read the following question and have your group either text in their answer to the leader or write responses on a note card and pass it anonymously to the leader.

> **What are the markers of a super Christian?**

Next, the group leader should read each response one at a time. Have group members vote on who they think each answer belongs to. Group members will earn one point for every correct guess they make. They will lose one point for each person who correctly guesses their response. Have fun!

> **Were there common threads among some of the answers?**

> **Was there a specific outlier that you hadn't considered before?**

Each of us likely has a picture in our minds of what we think supreme faith and followership of Jesus is supposed to look like. That picture may make you uncomfortable or may feel like an unattainable goal when it comes to spiritual growth. Maybe you're nervous praying out loud. Maybe Sunday morning handshakes send your germaphobic tendencies into orbit. Maybe raising your hands in worship feels awkward. Maybe the subject of missions doesn't make you tingly and the thought of traveling overseas doesn't whet your spiritual appetite. Hard truth: each of these things is connected to an outward display of religion and isn't necessarily an indication of a deep relationship with God. James wrote that justice—specifically for orphans and widows—is the purest portrayal of right religion (see Jas. 1:27).

GROUP

DISCUSS
Discuss the following bullet points.

- Define *justice*.
- Identify specific needs or people groups in need within your context.
- Discuss ways your church engages hurting people in your community.

Does a discussion about real justice scare you? Why or why not?

What are things you believe God might call you to do that you feel personally unprepared for, are unwilling to do, or are undeserving of your attention?

It was true then and it's true now. The most vulnerable people are those with no one to love or care for them. Kids without parents and women mourning loss are among the most at-risk people in our world today. They often suffer from poverty, sickness, and even abuse. It's those very people whom Scripture commands we reach out to. James wasn't offering his audience something new as a matter of their worship practice. He's reminding them of something very old, the heart of God as described by God's Word.

> ¹² *I delivered the poor who cried for help, and the fatherless who had none to help him.* ¹³ *The blessing of him who was about to perish came upon me, and I caused the widow's heart to sing for joy.* ¹⁴ *I put on righteousness, and it clothed me; my justice was like a robe and a turban.* ¹⁵ *I was eyes to the blind and feet to the lame.* ¹⁶ *I was a father to the needy, and I searched out the cause of him whom I did not know.*
> JOB 29:12-16, ESV

Who are the vulnerable people in need listed in this passage?

Job refers to justice as a robe and turban that he puts on. Job is saying that he wears justice. He puts it on everyday. He lives with a social consciousness. The vulnerable are always on his mind and in his heart. His lifestyle reflects the character of God. Plainly put, it was obvious and easy to spot the kind of man Job was.

Do you feel the kind of life Job described is an attainable goal for you? Explain.

Spiritual maturity isn't just something you do with your mind. It's about how you live your life. One of the saddest indications of failure in the area of justice and mercy is our description of those who excel in doing justice. We describe them as radical, extraordinary. Yet as we read the Bible together, we find that it treats issues of mercy and justice as anything but extraordinary. Frankly, doing justice is just a normal part of the Christian life. It's really easy to become part of a super-Christian subculture, comfortably embracing sensationalism. You can listen to Christian music, keep up with the latest Christian podcasts, and read Christian authors. You can engage in multiple Bible studies and serve on ministry teams, all the while never actually touching one of Scripture's defining characteristics of God-honoring faith: justice.

Close your group time by reading Micah 6:8 aloud together.

> **Mankind, He has told you what is good**
> **and what it is the LORD requires of you:**
> **to act justly,**
> **to love faithfulness,**
> **and to walk humbly with your God.**

This journey will expose what ordinary justice looks like and invite you to become who God created you to be in Christ. It will challenge you to follows Jesus daily and become what Job described as "eyes for the blind and feet to the lame" (Job 29:15). Maybe that's what we mean when we say we hope to be the hands and feet of Christ.

What are opportunities you have had to step up and be Christ to people in need?

APPLY

Knowing is really only half the battle. The other half is doing. As a group, commit to the following opportunities that lie ahead.

- Make Micah 6:8 your life verse for the next few weeks. Commit it to memory as you embark on this important journey of making ordinary faith a reality in your life.

- Commit to the activities outlined in each of the Action pages over the weeks ahead. The Action pages of this guide along with the individual-study portion provide an opportunity to solidify your move toward living a life of everyday, ordinary justice. It's a chance to look at your wardrobe and make sure you are clothed in God's justice.

Video sessions available for purchase at *lifeway.com/ordinary* or for streaming with a subscription to *smallgroup.com*

ACTION

SYMPATHY IS NO SUBSTITUTE FOR ACTION.

As a group, take time to discuss your typical weekly schedules. There are no bonus points for the busiest group members. Just be honest about where you steward your time each week:

- Amount of time you spend at work or in class
- Amount of time you spend recreationally and socially
- Amount of time you spend in prayer, Bible study, and corporate worship experiences
- Amount of time remaining

Considering the time you have, is there anything in your life that can be cut or recrafted to allow for more missional margin? While it is important to reprioritize and rebudget your schedule from time to time, that's really a peripheral purpose to this study.

Ordinary justice isn't about adding another thing to an already tight schedule. It's about leveraging the everyday moments of normal life and daily routine to offer Christlike hope to the world.

Talk about ways you can be mindful of justice in each of following areas of life:
- Work/class
- Recreationally/socially
- Worship/Bible study
- Other

Becoming an ordinary Christian won't happen overnight, so take small steps. And it won't be a solo endeavor either. Seek out two or three people in your group to be more intentional with. You may even want to ask someone not doing this study to come along on this journey with you. Commit to pray for them daily and meet with them weekly to discuss what you are learning as part of this Bible study experience.

Finally, revisit your list of local needs (the one you composed with your group as part of the discussion on page 8). Store that list in your phone. Make it your desktop background on your computer. Just make sure it's in a prominent place where you will see it regularly.

INDIVIDUAL-STUDY OVERVIEW

When was your last vacation? Vacations are a chance to refuel and refocus on what is important. Planned well, vacations can be like Sabbath. Consider this individual study to be a bit like a vacation. The moments you dedicate to this individual-study time can provide the quiet you need in your life to hear the voice of God. These personal moments can offer you the necessary distance from daily life to gain godly perspective and make intentional steps toward Christlike living.

This week's individual study examines key Old Testament passages with which James' Jewish audience would have been familiar. The idea of justice for vulnerable people was not new to them, but one that had been ignored. James' cry was for followers of Christ to bear fruit consistent with Christ. That is our hope as well—that our lives would look ever more like Christ, that intensely following Him would be our everyday, ordinary way of life.

PRAY

Ask God to reveal spiritual blind spots in the lives of group members that may be keeping them from seeing where Christ is leading. Ask the Holy Spirit to guide and direct each member toward opportunities that expand perspective and invite action.

ORDINARY JUSTICE ISN'T ABOUT ADDING ANOTHER THING TO AN ALREADY TIGHT SCHEDULE. IT'S ABOUT LEVERAGING THE EVERYDAY MOMENTS OF NORMAL LIFE AND DAILY ROUTINE TO OFFER CHRISTLIKE HOPE TO THE WORLD.

DOING JUSTICE IS JUST A NORMAL PART OF THE
CHRISTIAN LIFE. ORDINARY PEOPLE, DOING ORDINARY
THINGS, TURNING THE WORLD UPSIDE DOWN.

SELECTIVE SCRIPTURING

Christlikeness should be commonplace for the Christian, right? It depends on a person's definition of Christlikeness and the sources from which their description is drawn. Thomas Jefferson created his own version of Scripture by carefully cutting passages from his copy of the New Testament and pasting them into his own account. Largely committed to the specific moral teachings of Jesus, Jefferson omitted sections pertaining to miracles and occurrences that argued against reason.

Before you speak ill of the deceased or berate Jefferson for picking and choosing which parts of the biblical text mattered and which parts didn't, take a look in the mirror. Aren't many of the problems we face today in part because of our own proclivity to follow what we like from Scripture and conveniently ignore what we don't?

> Are there parts of Scripture or even the Christian life in general you find difficult? List them below.

Selective Scripture reading isn't a product of the American Revolution or our own postmodern landscape. Look at the challenges facing Jesus:

> *60 When many of His disciples heard this, they said, "This teaching is hard! Who can accept it?" 66 From that moment many of His disciples turned back and no longer accompanied Him.*
> JOHN 6:60,66

> *42 Nevertheless, many did believe in Him even among the rulers, but because of the Pharisees they did not confess Him, so they would not be banned from the synagogue. 43 For they loved praise from men more than praise from God.*
> JOHN 12:42-43

Jesus experienced attrition in His earthly ministry. At some point the teaching became too difficult or the cost became too great.

Compose a list of common characteristics of following Jesus.

Of those items on your list, which are perceived as difficult or sacrificial? Why?

For many in the Gospel narratives, following Jesus was costly. Nicodemus sought Jesus in the middle of the night because of his status as a Pharisee (see John 3). A scribe sought to follow Jesus but was alerted to the truth of having no home. Still another came, but learned it would be at the expense of his family (see Matt. 8:18-22). Jesus also explained to His followers that carrying a cross would eventually be the path of discipleship (see Matt. 16:24). The promise of an easy, consequence-free life for the Christ follower is nonexistent. In fact, we're told that we'll be hated for the cause of Christ (see Matt. 10:22). A quick summary statement for Christianity might be: *Becoming a Christian is easy. Being a Christ follower is hard. The former requires only faith. The latter? Everything else.*

That could even be utilized as a warning label: "Enter at your own risk." Following Jesus does mean hard teaching. A Christlike understanding of justice is no exception.

Read Matthew 23:14,23-24. What are some of your observations from this passage?

To be a Pharisee, according to Jesus, was to be categorized as someone who didn't practice what he preached. Hypocrites. Liars. Oppressors. According to Matthew 23:4, the burden of religion imposed by the Pharisees was heavy. It was extrabiblical legalism that didn't matter. They ignored important commands of God like justice, mercy, and faith but pressed hard on handwashing, public prayers, and careful tithing. Consider the matters of spirituality, religion, or worship that take up space in your life. Are they the things that God desires or that tradition imposes?

Can you think of things that tradition has etched on your mind but may not really reflect God's heart and will for your life? Journal your thoughts below.

LOWEST COMMON DENOMINATOR

In math, fractions represent parts of a whole. The challenge for any young mathematician is finding what's known as the lowest or least common denominator. That's the number of which both the numerators in the fraction are multiples.

$$1/2 = 3/6 = 6/12 = 12/24$$

The goal of finding the lowest common denominator or least common multiple is the ability to add, subtract, and manipulate fractions. Without finding the least common denominator for the bottom half of a fraction, you can't easily determine that ½ + ¼ = ¾ or much of anything else related to parts of a whole.

In following Christ, many of us seem to be searching for the lowest common denominator. What's the lowest hanging fruit when it comes to our connection with other believers in our churches? Is it knowing and being able to recite what's commonly called the Lord's Prayer? Is it average church attendance? Small-group participation? Tithing? Singing songs? Celebrating Christmas or Easter?

Perhaps you're accustomed to a community of faith where common, ordinary believers participate in church life but missions and sacrificial living are reserved for an elite group of called Christians like pastors and missionaries.

The call of the ordinary Christian is to understand that the burden of Christ and the responsibility for the least, last, and lost of the world isn't issued to a few elite, extraordinary Christians. It's the command for all believers in Jesus.

With regard to a least common denominator, we would be better suited to look for the highest possible calling.

You already spent time as a group considering markers of "super-Christianity." Now, name a few bare minimum common denominators of what it means to follow Christ. In other words, what are the most basic actions that should be true of all believers?

Religion that pleases God the Father must be pure and spotless. You must help needy orphans and widows and not let this world make you evil.
JAMES 1:27, CEV

Do your lowest common denominators of Christianity make our Father happy? The prophet Amos had something to say about that to the people of Israel:

> **21** *I hate, I despise your feasts!*
> *I can't stand the stench*
> *of your solemn assemblies.*
> **22** *Even if you offer Me*
> *your burnt offerings and grain offerings,*
> *I will not accept them;*
> *I will have no regard*
> *for your fellowship offerings of fattened cattle.*
> **23** *Take away from Me the noise of your songs!*
> *I will not listen to the music of your harps.*
> **24** *But let justice flow like water,*
> *and righteousness, like an unfailing stream.*
> AMOS 5:21-24

James was right. Religion that God accepts isn't ceremony and ritual, in spite of the prescriptions He gave Israel for those very practices. The religion God accepts is the religion of the heart. It's the religion of loving people the way He loves them.

Amos wasn't suggesting that they no longer participate in traditional worship gatherings or practices. James never suggested that we stop gathering, singing, studying, or praying. However, both prophetic voices are asserting that without justice those worship practices don't matter.

Jesus seemed to be in agreement in His words to the Pharisees:

> **23** *Woe to you, scribes and Pharisees, hypocrites! You pay a tenth of mint, dill, and cumin, yet you have neglected the more important matters of the law—justice, mercy, and faith. These things should have been done without neglecting the others.* **24** *Blind guides! You strain out a gnat, yet gulp down a camel!*
> MATTHEW 23:23-24

The Pharisees of Jesus' day were the class of professional Jews. Yet Jesus admonished them because of their hypocrisy. Their hearts didn't match their heads. Their words weren't authenticated by compassionate lives. For Jesus, it wasn't either/or. It was both/and.

Searching for the lowest common denominator in matters of faith is like looking for the easiest way to get by with the least amount of effort. In our pursuit of Christ, getting by can't be the goal. Honoring God must be the supreme aim.

Pause now and offer God a heartfelt prayer of commitment. Commit to God your desire to give Him your best, rather than your least.

GOD-SIZED CARE

One of the ways we administer justice is the manner in which we administer justice to the world. We do it best by illustrating God-sized care for the world in need.

Job knew a bit about God's blessing. Why? Because he had it and then lost it. Think back to the leanest moment of your life. Was it the efficiency apartment you had in college? Was it a pantry full of ramen noodles? Was it your first year as a married couple trying to navigate new jobs and new budgets? Was it when your company had corporate layoffs? One of the best ways to appreciate stability and provision is to live in a season where both of those blessings are up in the air.

Describe your leanest moment in life so far.

> RELIGION THAT PLEASES GOD THE FATHER MUST BE PURE AND SPOTLESS. YOU MUST HELP NEEDY ORPHANS AND WIDOWS AND NOT LET THIS WORLD MAKE YOU EVIL.
> **JAMES 1:27, CEV**

Satan, the accuser, was certain that if God removed Job's financial means, family status, and personal health, Job would deny God (see Job 1:11; 2:5). So God allowed it all, and Job didn't blame or deny Him (see Job 1:22; 2:10). Job understood that God's name was to be praised when He gave and also when He took away (see Job 1:21).

Later in the poetic piece we know as the Book of Job, readers uncover these words defining justice. It really is a God-sized care passage.

> ¹⁶ *If I have refused the wishes of the poor*
> *or let the widow's eyes go blind,*
> ¹⁷ *if I have eaten my few crumbs alone*
> *without letting the fatherless eat any of it—*
> ¹⁸ *for from my youth, I raised him as his father,*
> *and since the day I was born I guided the widow—*
> ¹⁹ *if I have seen anyone dying for lack of clothing*
> *or a needy person without a cloak,*
> ²⁰ *if he did not bless me*
> *while warming himself with the fleece from my sheep,*
> ²¹ *if I ever cast my vote against a fatherless child*
> *when I saw that I had support in the city gate,*
> ²² *then let my shoulder blade fall from my back,*
> *and my arm be pulled from its socket.*
> JOB 31:16-22

Job was becoming more aggressive in his attempt to clear his name. His contemporaries presumed that Job's predicament came as the result of disobedient or unjust living (see Job 22:4-11). Although the context for this passage is more closely tied to why suffering exists and whether sin leads to loss, it's also an easy passage to glean proper definitions concerning Godly compassion.

Name the vulnerable people outlined by Job's testimony in this passage.

Underline the specific needs mentioned by Job in this response.
How seriously did Job seem to take the responsibility to care for people in these points of need?

How do you come in contact with any or all of these in your everyday life?

One reason God-sized care may not be part of your ordinary Christian life is that you're insulated from the God-sized problems of the world. You can likely name a famous pastor or Christian artist/musician. But can you name an orphan? You're probably familiar with the writings of C. S. Lewis. But are you familiar with the location of the highest concentration of homeless people in your community?

The problem with ...

- the trafficked orphan girl in Moldova,
- the HIV-positive single mom in sub-Saharan Africa,
- the child soldier in Sierra Leone,
- and the family with no food or clean water in Honduras

... is that they don't live next door.

We can dismiss them as distant problems rather than see them as neighbors in need. What we don't see or experience, we can compartmentalize and ignore. Ultimately, it's a misinterpretation of a children's Sunday school lesson—the good Samaritan (see Luke 10:25-37). In response to an expert interview, Jesus taught us that everyone is a neighbor. Through the parable, Jesus instructs us to be aware of people's needs. Because the injured party was ignored by the very people who should have easily integrated the law into their lives (a priest and a Levite) and was finally cared for by a Samaritan (arch enemies of the Jews), the story struck a chord.

Do you find it easy to become impassioned for the cause of global justice or easy to ignore? What about local justice?

What parts of your schedule can put justice in the back seat of your life?

Are there people who model "Good Samaritanship" in your life? Who stands out and why?

We also live in the age of non-profit professionalization. There are amazing agencies performing incredible acts of relief in the world. Outside of all the international legalities, there is a key benefit of supporting such agencies. Pooling the resources of many people can make a much larger impact. There's also a key downside. Debiting $30 a month to feed a child in the developing world is fantastic. It's also really low involvement. It doesn't have to translate into a life that sees and meets needs in a personal, hands-on way. It can offer an out when it comes to getting dirty, building relationships, and physically meeting a person's needs.

Also, the invitation to share God's passion for people isn't just about taking trips around the world. It's about being aware of needs in your own community.

Take a moment to pray and ask God to open your eyes to various needs and to pour Himself and His God-sized ability to care into your heart.

REDEMPTION AND RESTORATION
When we were slaves to sin, God freed us. When we were orphans with no hope, He adopted us. When we were sojourners with no home, He welcomed us. When we were widows, His Son became our groom. God's mercy and justice flow from the cross. That's where we meet God and have redemption.

In an effort to communicate salvation and teach about the coming kingdom, Jesus offered a series of references to the types of people who would inherit eternal life. Wise virgins, faithful servants, and ministry-minded sheep (see Matt. 25).

Read Matthew 25:21-46 from your Bible and then focus in on verses 34-36 printed below.

34 Then the King will say to those on His right, "Come, you who are blessed by My Father, inherit the kingdom prepared for you from the foundation of the world.

35 For I was hungry
and you gave Me something to eat;
I was thirsty
and you gave Me something to drink;
I was a stranger and you took Me in;
36 I was naked and you clothed Me;
I was sick and you took care of Me;
I was in prison and you visited Me."
MATTHEW 25:34-36

Ultimately, Jesus gave us His own life as bread (see John 6:35) that will always make us full and water that will always quench our thirst (see John 4:14). Jesus' blood afforded us forgiveness, which leads to adoption and, ultimately, purpose. He made us His own and He is the very essence of our lives (see Col. 3:4).

It's odd to think that we could feed, clothe, welcome, nurture, visit, etc. the maker of all things. Jesus asserts that when we meet the needs of someone considered least, we're offering it unto Him (see Matt. 25:40).

Describe a time when you felt like "one of the least of these" in your own life.

Did someone step up and meet a need? In what way? How did you feel?

Consider any "least of these" situations that might be present in your circle of influence right now. How can you step up and meet a need in your current community (food, clothing, care, attention)?

Read the following verses from Ephesians and respond to the question that follows.

> *7 We have redemption in Him through His blood, the forgiveness of our trespasses, according to the riches of His grace 8 that He lavished on us with all wisdom and understanding.*
>
> EPHESIANS 1:7-8

How is Christ's blood related to redemption?

In this Ephesians passage, Paul writes about redemption through the blood of Jesus. What he means is ransom money paid to God for the release of a person's debt. That debt is caused by sin. And it's a debt none of us could ever afford on our own.

It's through Christ that we have redemption. Christ lived the perfect life of righteousness that we could never live and then died the death that we deserved to die. Through His sacrifice, our lives are redeemed and made righteous before God. Because of the power of Jesus now alive in us, we too can live out the righteousness and justice of God. It's our right response to the forgiveness we've been given. Here's how Timothy Keller put it:

> *If a person has grasped the meaning of God's grace in his heart, he will do justice. If he doesn't live justly, then he may say with his lips that he is grateful for God's grace, but in his heart he is far from him. If he doesn't care about the poor, it reveals that at best he doesn't understand the grace he has experienced, and at worst he has not really encountered the saving mercy of God. Grace should make you just.[1]*

An irresponsible reading of Matthew 25 might lead someone to believe that we earn a place in God's kingdom through justice-wielding good works. Feeding the hungry. Clothing the naked. Tending the sick. Visiting the lonely. Earning God's favor. God's grace is still present in this passage. After all, the sheep are inheriting the kingdom that has been "prepared for them from the foundation of the world" (v. 34). That's a clear indicator of God's grace. It's His generosity that affords us His kingdom. The truth is that the works indicated by Jesus in this parable are in response to the grace already received.

BECAUSE OF THE POWER OF JESUS NOW ALIVE IN US, WE TOO CAN LIVE OUT THE RIGHTEOUSNESS AND JUSTICE OF GOD. IT'S OUR RIGHT RESPONSE TO THE FORGIVENESS WE'VE BEEN GIVEN.

How have you seen God's grace alive in your life?

How have you experienced His providential hand of blessing? Be specific.

One day Christ will return and His kingdom will be restored. There will no longer be a need for justice because there will no longer be a "least of these" part of the population in need of it. Being a justice-minded Christ follower today is about demonstrating Christ's future reality in your present context.

How does doing unto "the least of these" communicate Christ to people?

Have you ever experienced someone come to faith in Christ in the context of a Matthew 25 moment (i.e. being fed, clothed, cared for, loved, etc.)? Explain.

How is meeting the demands of justice a good front door to share the gospel message of Jesus?

How do you perceive a healthy perspective on justice to be related to God's plan of redemption?

MOVING TOWARD ACTION

Each week your individual study will include a final section called "Moving Toward Action." Use this final section to solidify your action steps toward justice. Remember, the idea of being a justice-minded Christ follower isn't a pressure to add another item to your daily to-do list. It's an opportunity to infuse more Christlikeness into who you already are.

In Matthew 7:24-28 Jesus described two types of builders—wise and foolish. Wise men build houses on solid foundations. Foolish men don't. Connecting the dots, Jesus explained that anyone who hears His words and puts them into action is like a wise builder. Those who hear His words and ignore them might as well construct a house on sand. Both homes will face storms, but only one will remain standing. The same is true in the lives of people. We will all face incredible odds. But only wise listeners will stand strong.

When it comes to God's Word, application is essential. A fool can know God's Word inside and out, but if he doesn't heed it, he remains a fool. Engaging a Bible study like this and not being moved to action is the mark of a foolish builder. Wisdom calls you to practice this portion of your faith. That said, how will ordinary justice make its way into your skin and out through your hands and feet?

Justice is often viewed as an extra-credit option, a distraction, or something to ignore all together. But those who have a high view of God, His Word, and justification by faith should be leading the way in administering God's justice to the world.

Set three goals regarding missional living this week. How can you infuse justice into your everyday life? Categorize them by seeing, hearing, and doing.

Seeing

Hearing

Doing

Hearing and listening can be interchangeably used in some cases, but not all. Hearing can be simple observation. Listening means letting something really sink in. Revisit some of the Scriptures you have studied this week. In the space provided, write a one-sentence summary or action step based on that particular passage.

James 1:27

Matthew 23:14,23-24

Amos 5:21-24

Job 31:16-22

Luke 10:25-37

Choose one of the needs you have noticed in your local community and meet it. Make it something you can realistically tackle this week. The point is to exercise God's call *on* your life to let justice flow *out* of your life.

List your goals for meeting this need.

When you have met this need, journal your experience here.

PRAYER

As a matter of prayer this week, make your own humble confession before God.

- In what ways have you ignored the commands in His Word?

- In what ways have you ignored the needs of the world?

- In what ways do you hope to better integrate His Word into your ordinary life, thereby, better illustrating Him to the world?

- Ask God to open your eyes and ears to see needs.

- Ask Him to give you a heart of compassion to actively pursue ways to meet the needs He reveals.

MANKIND,
HE HAS TOLD
YOU WHAT
IS GOOD
AND WHAT
IT IS THE
LORD REQUIRES
OF YOU:
TO ACT JUSTLY,
TO LOVE
FAITHFULNESS,
AND TO WALK
HUMBLY WITH
YOUR GOD.

MICAH 6:8

1. Timothy Keller, *Generous Justice: How God's Grace Makes Us Just* (New York: Riverhead, 2010), 68.

NEIGHBOR LOVE

HOW JUSTIFIED SINNERS SHOW COMPASSION IN WORD AND DEED

View video session 2 as a group and then dive into the discussion guide below.

OPEN

Test your singing ability in this fun group challenge. Gather in a circle. Moving clockwise, everyone must sing a title or line from a song that contains the word *love*. Songs cannot be repeated and play must move quickly around the circle. A player is out if he or she fails to sing a line with the word "love," repeats a previous song, hesitates, or forfeits because he or she can't produce anything new.

Allow the last two players to battle it out until you declare a winner.

Why do you think love is such a key feature in popular music?

There's no shortage of songs about love. You could play this game all night and only be limited by your own interest and knowledge. If songwriters are the poets and theologians of culture, then one thing is for sure: everyone is interested in love. Unfortunately, many confuse love with other things.

Divide your group into four teams. Assign each team a term from the list below. If you don't have enough people for four teams, you can divide the group in half and give each group two terms. Each group is to define their assigned word(s) and then share a manner in which culture confuses that word with love.

- Tolerance
- Romance
- Affinity
- Sentimentalism

GROUP

DISCUSS

In order to dissect and truly understand love, particularly as it pertains to living a life of biblical justice, we must dive into what Scripture says love is. First, the Bible tells us that "God is love" (1 John 4:8). Beyond that, we could ask a series of follow-up questions and still land right back where we started. "What does love look like?" "What does love do?" "How is love distributed?"

Read 1 John 3:16.

> **According to this verse, how do we know what love truly is?**

> **What should that recognition of love cause us to do?**

John writes that we don't have to guess about love. There is a way to tell what love is, and it starts with the manner in which Jesus loved. Jesus' love wasn't a mystical, philosophical, or sentimental love. Jesus' love was an active love. He didn't merely say He "loved." He demonstrated love. His greatest act of love was on the cross. Paul wrote, "God proves His own love for us in that while we were still sinners, Christ died for us!" (Rom. 5:8).

> **If tangible love equals sacrificial love, how do you show it to the people who are important to you?**

> **How do those people show *you* sacrificial love?**

Consider this definition of love: *Love is compassion that leads to action.*

> **Unpack this definition as a group. Do you agree or disagree? Is it complete or does it lack an important aspect about love? Can it be applied generally to all relationships or is it too narrow in focus?**

> **While the ultimate display happened on a cross, Jesus illustrated true love in many other ways. What were some of those ways?**

Read Luke 10:25-29.

These verses are the on-ramp for the parable Jesus told regarding the good Samaritan.

> **Summarize this parable as a group.**

Now read Luke 10:30-37.

In verse 33 of the parable, Jesus said that the Samaritan had compassion. Jesus told this story to get the attention of His listeners. None of the Jews within earshot would have welcomed the idea of a Samaritan being the hero. Jesus could have just responded to the legal expert's question "Who is my neighbor?" by saying, "Everyone everywhere." But He didn't. He took it a step further. The parable of the injured man being ignored and then rescued communicates to us that all of humanity is a neighbor whom we are to love. That's not all Jesus taught though. He also provided a recipe for what it means to show all of humanity sacrificial love.

> In order for the Samaritan traveler to show love, what did it require of him?

> If compassion leads to action, what are ways we should be showing love and claiming justice for people in need?

To be a good Samaritan means embracing the idea of mercy ministry. Mercy equals compassion. Ministry is active and involved. To engage mercy ministry is to leverage gifts, time, resources, and ideas in order to show the world compassion in tangible, life-changing ways.

APPLY

Discuss the following question:

> Is it more important to meet a person's physical need or share the gospel of Christ? Explain.

Ultimately, the answer to that question is both. One is not more important than the other. Both are paramount. While many may want to separate sharing the good news of hope in Jesus from addressing needs in a clearly broken world, it's not neighborly love to choose one over the other. Nor is it a safe assumption that either can carry with it the context of the other.

> Do you tend to lean more toward one way of demonstrating love than the other? Explain.

> How can we better become a people who do both/and rather than either/or when it comes to justice-minded, sacrificial love?

Video sessions available for purchase at *lifeway.com/ordinary* or for streaming with a subscription to *smallgroup.com*

ACTION

"GO AND DO LIKEWISE." JESUS, LUKE 10:37

Take a few quiet moments to reflect as you close your group time this week and prepare to take action.

Group leaders, read aloud the following prompts. Participants, as each prompt is read, silently consider who in your life fits the description. Or you may jot a name in the space provided.

> Who is a person in your neighborhood you don't know? You may wave politely and nod when seeing him or her. Perhaps you had a conversation once by the mailbox but haven't really spoken in months. You don't know what this neighbor does, if Christ is real to him or her, or any of this person's wounds, joys, or goals.

> Who do you know personally that is hurting? Who has just experienced loss? Who needs a friend, but it will require much? Grief. Pain. Disappointment. Dissatisfaction. Who in your life needs a genuine reach because of present circumstances?

> Who is your enemy? This is someone difficult to love. Everything about this person disturbs your day and your disposition. He or she personifies pet peeve to you. With whom is that conflict you try to ignore but feel like the problem won't go away? Maybe someone who needs your forgiveness.

According to God's Word, we're called to love neighbors, the least of these, and our enemies. Jesus' life and death exemplifies such love, and once a person receives salvation in Christ, then the Spirit empowers such love. Christ loved His brothers; He loved His neighbor; He loved the least of these; and He loved His enemies. In Jesus, we know what love is; it's the ordinary expression of one neighbor to another.

Talk about a few tangible ways you can show love to the people you thought of when you read the descriptions above. What actions can you take this week? The actions should be simple and reproducible. They should involve effort and sacrifice. They should channel Jesus and the manner in which He loved— simply but completely.

Last session you created a smaller group of people to touch base with weekly about your ordinary journey. This week when you gather, talk about your progress toward reaching out and loving the people you thought of during the group time today.

INDIVIDUAL-STUDY OVERVIEW

This week's individual study is an opportunity to further unpack the parable of the good Samaritan. Beyond the sacrificial love the Samaritan traveler displayed and the definition of a neighbor that Jesus provided, there are some theological tensions in the text that you may not have considered before. Enjoy your personal study time. Enter into it with an attitude of emptiness, asking Christ to fill you as you spend time with Him this week.

PRAY

Thank God for His perfect love. Ask Him to birth that kind of love for the world in you.

CHRIST LOVED HIS BROTHERS; HE LOVED HIS NEIGHBOR; HE LOVED THE LEAST OF THESE; AND HE LOVED HIS ENEMIES. IN JESUS, WE KNOW WHAT LOVE IS; IT'S THE ORDINARY EXPRESSION OF ONE NEIGHBOR TO ANOTHER.

ONCE YOU REALIZE THAT YOU'VE BEEN FORGIVEN OF AN INFINITE DEBT, YOU'LL PRACTICE OPEN-HANDED GENEROSITY.

LAWYER TALK

Begin your individual-study time by reading Luke 10:25-37.

Numerous moments in Jesus' ministry were marked by accusation. Frequent testing came from religious leaders. Traps were set in order to catch Christ in a punishable action according to Jewish law and tradition. This moment was no different:

> **Just then an expert in the law stood up to test Him, saying, "Teacher, what must I do to inherit eternal life?"**
> LUKE 10:25

How did the Lord respond? Jesus pointed the lawyer back to Scripture and asked him to answer his own question. Deuteronomy 6:5 (love God) and Leviticus 19:18 (love others) were sufficient answers according to Jesus. These particular Old Testament verses are quoted elsewhere in the New Testament and also by Jesus Himself (see Matt. 22:34-40). But as you know, it is never enough to just know the right answer.

Next, the lawyer looked for a loophole. If he could minimize the definition of the word *neighbor*, he could lessen the restrictions and make them more manageable.

Why do you think the lawyer wanted restrictions he could manage on his own?

The purpose of this parable wasn't to indicate that the lawyer could achieve salvation by roadside assistance or any other kind of service operation. If the story Jesus told ignited a passion for the lawyer to pursue righteousness by works to a higher degree than he already did, the message would have promoted a false theology inconsistent with the true gospel message.

If Jesus had provided a response to either question—"What must I do to inherit eternal life?" or "Who is my neighbor?"—then salvation wouldn't be necessary. The presence of sin means we need grace. True grace does for man what he cannot possibly do for himself. Anyone operating with a self-righteous disposition like this lawyer is either under the impression that his sin isn't bad enough or that his works can somehow be good enough.

> Which one of these are you most likely to believe: that your sin isn't bad enough or that your works can somehow be good enough? Explain why you answered that way.

In one sense the story of the good Samaritan sets a high goal for us in how we show love. It expands our view of just who our neighbor is and how far our neighborhood borders actually extend. But it does something more. In exposing the lawyer's inner racism toward Samaritans, Jesus taught that everyone, including one's own enemies, falls in the category of those we are to love as our neighbors. Such a high standard of love should make anyone cry out, "Have mercy on me a sinner!"

Before we can be justice-minded believers who demonstrate a high degree of neighborly love, we must first come to terms with the fact that true love extends far beyond the degree that someone is able to earn it.

Salvation is a gift. We didn't get it even in part because of our likability. It's a challenge to put ourselves in the spot of the good Samaritan. But that is the type of love we're called to show. It's much easier to place ourselves in the sandals of another character in the story—the injured man. Ultimately, Jesus is the Great Samaritan and each of us is the traveler left for dead, in need of a Savior.

> How does that mental picture shape your perspective on this parable?

How does the intense love and rescue Jesus provided you motivate the manner in which you love others?

Read 1 John 4:19.

Why are we able to show love to others? Does this make it easier or more difficult to love? Explain.

Getting back in touch with the free, totally undeserved gift of God's dramatic love is a reminder of both why and how we are to love others. The Samaritan didn't stop to help because the man on the road was good. He did it because he was good. That goodness is inspiring.

WORD AND DEED

One of the reasons the gospel is so compelling and so believable is that Jesus didn't just teach us how to live and follow God. He showed us. The world is waiting for that beautiful picture to be demonstrated by each generation. We don't just show love in word. We don't just show love in deed. We show love in word *and* deed.

It's true that we are justified by faith alone, but the faith that saves is never alone. Saving faith is an active faith. God's people are about God's business.

Although we are condemned by the evil deeds we do, our good deeds don't save us. In response to the good grace of God that saw fit to save us in spite of our sin, the believer who has been justified by that grace should be instinctively engaged in good deeds.

Read James 2:14-18.

How does James describe the relationship between faith and works in this passage?

A clear understanding of James' writing reveals that his perception of faith without works is that it is useless. Is it really the kind of faith that can save a man (see 2:14)? Conversely, dynamic faith is a faith that functions.

Now read Paul's words from Ephesians 2:8-10 and journal your thoughts as responses to these questions:

What are your initial reflections from this passage? Does it evoke any kind of emotion?

What do you perceive as the difference between the writings of Paul and James? What are the similarities?

Differences	Similarities

The call of the missionary believer is to take the Bible's message of justification by faith in Christ to the ends of the earth. You're called to leverage your job, your family, and your relationships so that others may know Christ. This is the call of every believer. This desire to spread the message of justification through faith is a call motivated by love—a desire for people to know and be freed by truth in the same manner we have been set free. Justice is also a call motivated by love. When it comes to global evangelism, justice says, "It is not right to keep the good news to ourselves when others have never heard it." The gospel is the cure for the worst of all diseases. If we really care about justice ministry, we will really care about taking the cure to the ends of the earth. Nearly half the world's people groups live where there is no gospel access. Half. Let that sink in. We need to make this our problem. We need to pray. And we need to go.

There are also those who only champion proclamation and discard mercy ministry. The places of greatest poverty and social need are often the places with the greatest need for gospel proclamation. The argument between gospel presentation and mercy ministry is a distraction. We simply need to go. When we get there, we should serve and speak in love.

How can serving someone in love and providing the mercy and justice of God in his or her life be an effective gospel-sharing tool?

IT'S TRUE THAT WE ARE JUSTIFIED BY FAITH ALONE, BUT THE FAITH THAT SAVES IS NEVER ALONE. SAVING FAITH IS AN ACTIVE FAITH. GOD'S PEOPLE ARE ABOUT GOD'S BUSINESS.

You can't do mercy ministry fueled by love without offering gospel hope for a changed life. You also can't speak a message of truth without addressing social needs. Alleviating temporary suffering is a tangible illustration of God's love, which relieves the demands of sin and eternal suffering.

Make a list of people in your life who need the gospel message of Jesus Christ. Who needs to know that they can be forgiven and free only by justification through faith?

Now list the people in your life with physical or emotional needs. Who needs to see the God of the lonely, hurt, vulnerable, and suffering in a tangible way?

Some relationships in your life may make both lists. They need your words and your deeds in order to see Christ. They may remain antagonistic to faith until they see an authentic witness for Christ that encompasses both what you say and how you serve.

FAMOUS LAST WORDS

Read Acts 20:18-21,35-38.

In the space provided, list what is important about each set of verses.

Acts 20:18-21

Acts 20:35-38

Paul is gearing up to board a ship sailing back home toward Jerusalem. In Acts 20, Paul is speaking to the Ephesian elders and explains his confidence that "chains and afflictions are waiting for me" in Jerusalem (Acts 20:23). Ultimately, he is transferred back to Rome where it's believed that the apostle died. Acts 20 records his last words to the church in Ephesus.

If you knew that life was nearing the end for you, what things would you want to communicate to others?

What things would you want to ensure that you did for people? Be specific with your answer.

What are the final words you would hope to say?

Knowing these were the last words he would speak to them in person, Paul paired two important parts of ministry life for us.

Paul was committed to preaching God's good news to people (see Acts 20:20). He also instructed them in the value of helping poor and weak people (see Acts 20:35). Communicating God's good news is an action birthed out of love for God and also love for others. Likewise, helping vulnerable people is an action birthed out of love for God and also love for people.

How do you think helping vulnerable people is an illustration of God's love and an important part of sharing the gospel?

In every way I've shown you that by laboring like this, it is necessary to help the weak and to keep in mind the words of the Lord Jesus, for He said, "It is more blessed to give than to receive."
ACTS 20:35

At the conclusion of his address, Paul quotes Jesus (see Acts 20:35). However, reading back through the Gospels, these words of Christ that Paul cited aren't present. Perhaps Paul is sharing a word common in Christendom. There are certainly not three full years of spoken words and occurrences provided to us in the four gospels, especially since so much of the synoptic books (Matthew, Mark, and Luke) are repetitive. So Jesus definitely did and said more than is recorded. This quote is either a common expression attributed to Jesus or something specific that Christ told Paul.

Describe ways you have come to believe that the words of Acts 20:35 are true—that it really is better to give than receive.

An enemy of neighbor love is cause-centered Christianity. It's easy to get excited about a cause but never actually do anything for a real person. Today it's popular to put on a wristband advocating for the enslaved or to wear a t-shirt pressing the need for clean water. That's all fine and good, but love isn't sentimentalism. Nor is it a cause. Love should be given a name.

What desperate neighbor do you love? With whom are you sharing God's message of hope in word and deed? Paul leveraged this last speech and his relationship with the Ephesians to communicate the importance of both in our lives.

Pray and ask God to identify everyday ways you can be about both sharing and serving. Each is an act of love to a neighbor.

MERCY MINISTRY

Go back to the story of the good Samaritan. Read specifically Luke 10:33-35.

List exactly what the Samaritan man did for the wounded traveler.

To live everyday, ordinary justice in an outflow of love means to get personally involved. Mercy ministry is broad and involves effort. T-shirts and wristbands aren't enough. They may create awareness, but they don't provide justice—at least not in the direct way demonstrated by the Samaritan.

Mercy ministry good Samaritan style will take your time. Your compassion. Your money. Your effort. Your wisdom. And more.

The list below contains some of the ways you might be called to administer mercy and justice by rolling up your sleeves, getting dirty, staying with, providing for, and ultimately showing neighborly love.

- Supporting single mothers
- Defending vulnerable widows (especially in poor areas of the world)
- Caring for orphans
- Feeding the hungry
- Praying with the dying
- Freeing the enslaved
- Giving medical care to the diseased
- Helping the unemployed
- Visiting prisoners
- Welcoming sojourners
- Counseling the abused
- Comforting the grieving
- Serving the elderly
- Caring for the mentally ill
- Tutoring the underprivileged
- Ministering to juvenile delinquents
- Caring for the disabled
- Welcoming internationals
- Ministering to the addicted
- Aiding victims of disaster
- Reforming broken social structures
- Doing aftercare for rescued victims of trafficking
- Fighting child labor, child pornography, and child prostitution
- Seeking racial reconciliation
- Bringing the gospel to the spiritually lost

Go through the list and underline the things you have been a part of in the past. Now circle the things you can easily and practically engage in over the next few days and weeks.

Reread Luke 10:30-33.

Each of the four characters in the story of the good Samaritan had something very basic in common. They were all found on the same road between Jericho and Jerusalem. No matter the reason, each man happened to be on the same path at nearly the same time.

Coincidence? Not one bit. This is a story that Jesus' audience could have imagined. It was likely something that had occurred before, robbers beating a traveler and then leaving him to die. Not only did the fictitious characters in the parable have something in common, the listeners had something in common as well. They could all relate to this story.

This illustration of everyday justice provided by Jesus is perfect for our context too. In this story, Jesus isn't instructing the lawyer to go across the globe and find hurting people. Jesus is saying that when you find hurting people right where you are, do something.

Who should you focus on? Jesus' parable is helpful for answering this question. This Samaritan cared for the person on his path. One church can't do everything, nor can any one person. But who is the dying man on your road? Who needs mercy? Such individuals are all around us. The writer of Proverbs says, "When it is in your power, don't withhold good from the one it belongs to" (Prov. 3:27). We can't do it all, but we can all do something for our neighbors.

We can learn one more lesson from the Samaritan. What does verse 33 offer as the reason the Samaritan stopped? What did he have that the other two religious travelers did not?

What if the Samaritan man had been trying to earn the favor of God?

> Are you sometimes motivated by a desire to earn God's love? If yes, how so?

LOVE ISN'T SENTIMENTALISM. NOR IS IT A CAUSE. LOVE SHOULD BE GIVEN A NAME.

What if the Samaritan had also been one of the original robbers? What if he left the gang and came back to help the injured man because of guilt?

> Have you ever been motivated to serve because of your own guilt? Explain.

God cares not only about our deeds; He cares about our motives as well. One may be motivated to do good in order to gain merit before God, to impress others, or a hundred other reasons. Guilt is often used to get people moving. Guilt can be a great initiator, but it is a poor sustainer. People eventually change the channel. They stop listening. Ultimately, we must be motivated by grace and not guilt.

There are two interpretations for what the Samaritan man actually represented.

Interpretation 1: A great, benevolent God who redeems and restores. Jesus came as a humble servant and not a conquering king. How fitting that the hero in this parable is equally surprising. The Jews of Jesus' day would have been reluctant to accept the idea of a good Samaritan. Almost as reluctant as they were to view a carpenter's son from Nazareth as God's Holy Messiah. Still, the Samaritan man had compassion just like Jesus.

Read Matthew 9:35-38.

What do you notice from this passage in regard to Jesus' compassion?

Interpretation 2: The Samaritan man was a sinner saved by grace offering loving-kindness across significant racial boundaries out of the overflow of God's love in his life. This is a likely interpretation because Jesus says, "Go and do likewise." Go and show that same level of care and concern. Go get dirty. Give of your resources. Stay the course and finish what you start. *Likewise* here is a broad term. Jesus meant for the audience to do the things the Samaritan man did for the reason he did them.

It wasn't guilt. It wasn't works. It wasn't to impress anyone else. It was compassion.

MOVING TOWARD ACTION

This "Moving Toward Action" section is to solidify your action steps toward justice. When it comes to loving our neighbors, two things matter most. Even more than what you do, it's how you do it and why you do it that count. As you engage the Seeing, Hearing, and Doing portions of this section, remember to let neighborly love be the umbrella by which you read and listen to God's desire for you.

Read 2 Corinthians 5:14-15.

Here Paul writes to give a reason for his ministry, "For Christ's love compels us" (v. 14). It isn't logic that prompts Paul's work. It isn't guilt or pity. It's not sensationalism or fame. It's not an effort to work for God's approval or for man's. It's Christ's love.

> List ways you have experienced Christ's love personally. Some will be general ways consistent with the manner in which God loves all people, even unbelievers. Others should be specific to the ways in which He has loved you well.

Each of the items on your list compels you. When it comes to motivation, loving others because we have been loved promotes a lifestyle of ordinary justice.

We would all do well to keep Deuteronomy 6:5 in mind. "Love the Lord your God with all your heart, with all your soul, and with all your strength." Jesus identifies this command as the greatest, even more important than loving others. In fact, it's out of a love for God that we love our neighbors. Now consider the verses that follow.

> *6 These words that I am giving you today are to be in your heart. 7 Repeat them to your children. Talk about them when you sit in your house and when you walk along the road, when you lie down and when you get up. 8 Bind them as a sign on your hand and let them be a symbol on your forehead. 9 Write them on the doorposts of your house and on your gates.*
> DEUTERONOMY 6:6-9

As you close this individual study, consider making this "Seeing/Hearing/Doing" section a family Bible study. In doing so you model justice and pass faith on to the next generation. If you don't have children you can still easily do this with your spouse or individually.

SEEING

Part of justice is simply being aware of needs around you. Make a list of 10 people who are currently a part of your life on a regular basis. Next to each name on your list, identify a way you can show him or her Christ's love—Encouragement? Prayer? Time? Accountability? Help in a way they can't help themselves? Forgiveness? Ask God to help you see a way to love them well.

1.

2.

3.

4.

5.

6.

7.

8.

9.

10.

HEARING

We hear God's words through Scripture. Something special happens when we read it aloud. Take a few moments this week to read each of the following verses out loud. Then, in the space beside each verse, summarize what it communicates about love.

1 John 4:19

1 John 4:7

Romans 5:8

Colossians 3:14

John 14:15

> FOR CHRIST'S LOVE COMPELS US, SINCE WE HAVE REACHED THIS CONCLUSION: IF ONE DIED FOR ALL, THEN ALL DIED.
>
> **2 CORINTHIANS 5:14**

DOING

Refer to the list you made in the Seeing section. Choose two or three individuals who need neighborly love this week and log a plan in the space provided for how you will show it. Hopefully God is broadening your understanding of justice to see that it isn't just people in the developing world who need you. It's the widow two doors down. It's the family from the soccer team in which the dad has been out of work for three months. It's the single mom from your office. It's the foster care family at church. It's the unbeliever who is teetering on the edge of spiritual conversations. Each needs a conversation about faith and an illustration of God's love through your act of justice-minded service.

PRAYER

Pray a prayer of thanksgiving this week. Go back through your "Hearing" list of all the ways you have been loved by God so well and thank Him for each of them. Also pray a prayer of commissioning over your own life and that of your family. Ask God to send you, use you, and allow you to be part of His justice mission in the world.

KINGDOM HOSPITALITY

HOW THE KING'S PEOPLE WELCOME OTHERS

View video session 3 as a group and then dive into the discussion guide below.

OPEN

Kick this week off with a few fun icebreaker questions about hospitality.

1. What is the best meal you ever ate?

2. If you could only eat one meal every day for the rest of your life, what would you choose? Why?

3. What's your best go-to meal for guests?

4. What's the best dish you ever prepared?

5. What's the worst dish you ever prepared?

There are few things more ordinary than a meal. Yet we calendar our weeks, schedule our days, and even line item our budgets with food prep. People pin dishes on Pinterest, share them on Facebook, and even photo them on Instagram. Meals matter. So does hospitality. Something as simple as a meal, when shared, can open the door to something extraordinary.

What does hospitality look like to you?

We need to see hospitality through the lens of Scripture. To do that, we must distinguish it from two terms with which hospitality is often unfairly linked—entertaining and fellowship.

On the surface, hospitality can seem synonymous with entertaining. However, entertaining is about impressing others while hospitality is about serving others. Entertaining can easily make much of the host while hospitality makes much of the guests. Entertaining can come off shallow and superficial while hospitality brings depth and authenticity.

The biblical act of fellowship *(koinonia)* happens among believers living in community. We desperately need that. The literal definition of *hospitality*, however, is "love for strangers." Hospitality is what we extend to outsiders, strangers, and anyone who finds him or herself in deep physical or spiritual need.

GROUP

DISCUSS

Jesus illustrated incredible hospitality. He came for the least, the last, and the lost. His dinner companions often included social outcasts and numerous reports throughout the Gospels give us glimpses of Jesus offering a divine level of hospitality. Why divine? Because only the unmerited favor of God would warrant His perfect Son communing with such sinners.

Read Matthew 9:10-13.

> **Why might eating with tax collectors have been considered so deplorable?**

> **Why do you think Jesus talked about being sick versus well in His description of sinners? What might His choice of illustration have communicated to people who heard Him that day?**

Jesus was often depicted in Luke coming from a meal, at a meal, or leaving a meal. Jesus came to serve, not be served. And He came to seek and save the lost. How did He do that? Often around the table, eating meals, engaging in life-changing teaching for the purposes of evangelism and discipleship.

> **Can you think of other examples from Scripture of how Jesus modeled hospitality?**

> **In what ways might God call us today to practice Christlike hospitality? Brainstorm as a group and compose a list together.**

One great example of Jesus' hospitality can be found in Luke 19 with a small man by the name of Zacchaeus.

As a group, summarize the story of Zacchaeus and then read Luke 19:9.

> *"Today salvation has come to this house,"* Jesus told him,
> *"because he too is a son of Abraham."*
> LUKE 19:9

Salvation didn't come because Jesus ate with Zacchaeus or because Zacchaeus, by birth, was a direct descendant of Abraham. Salvation came because an encounter with Jesus was life changing. The act of hospitality, communion, personal interaction with Jesus changed Zacchaeus's life on the inside and his behavior on the outside.

> [8] Above all, maintain an intense love for each other, since love covers a multitude of sins. [9] Be hospitable to one another without complaining. [10] Based on the gift each one has received, use it to serve others, as good managers of the varied grace of God. [11] If anyone speaks, it should be as one who speaks God's words; if anyone serves, it should be from the strength God provides, so that God may be glorified through Jesus Christ in everything. To Him belong the glory and the power forever and ever. Amen.
> 1 PETER 4:8-11

When we exhibit the same gentle spirit of hospitality, we have an opportunity to give God the glory He deserves.

What are your initial reflections from this passage on biblical hospitality?

Consider some of the reasons or excuses people give for not practicing hospitality. Most of them really double as reasons people don't feel comfortable entertaining. Is there an undercurrent in your own life that seems to be steering you more toward complaining than true hospitality? You'll have an opportunity to examine that in your own life through your individual-study time this week.

APPLY

Following Jesus includes following His practice of hospitality—joyous, authentic, generous, countercultural, and hope-filled hospitality. When Jesus says, "Come, follow Me," He isn't calling us to offer a class or start a program, but to follow His way of life. And that way includes opening up our homes and lives to others. That actually starts with opening our hearts.

This week's Action page challenges you to open your heart by crucifying anything in you that inhibits you from carrying out Christ's mission of transformational hospitality. Next, your individual study provides a recipe for combining opportunity with responsibility where biblical hospitality is concerned.

Video sessions available for purchase at *lifeway.com/ordinary* or for streaming with a subscription to *smallgroup.com*

ACTION

HOSPITALITY IS WAR.

Is hospitality a kind-spirited entry point into the life of the church or a frontline battle to demonstrate the goodness of God? Agree or disagree, the art of hospitality in homes, in restaurants, through conversations and relationships, in everyday life is the manner in which the gospel has been spread and continues to spread throughout the world.

Ultimately, missions doesn't involve doing sensational acts; it involves simple, ordinary acts done with a heart of love. "Most gospel ministry involves ordinary people doing ordinary things with gospel intentionality."[1]

Your action step this week is to eat meals, preferably three of them each day. Plan ahead and determine which meals you might intentionally leverage to show biblical hospitality to others.

Here are some people to specifically target and options for how you might be intentional with your approach.

- Invite your pastor and his family over for dinner or out to a restaurant. Lori Wilhite, founder of a women's leadership forum, says that pastors are often very lonely and their wives are especially vulnerable to loneliness.[2] A Barna study indicated "61 percent of the 627 senior pastors interviewed reported that they had 'few close friends.'"[3] How might you offer ministry to one called to be a minister?
- Carve out time for lunch or afternoon coffee with a coworker or friend caught in struggle. Who is having trouble in his or her marriage? Who has a wayward child? Who is struggling with infertility? Who recently lost an aging parent? Consider all the elements in life you would note as painful or stressful and open your eyes to people around you facing those very things. How can your time and listening ear show another person how much God cares?
- On the run? Take a sack lunch to a local homeless person, one you typically drive by a few times each week. Better yet, be proactive and take his or her order before making the purchase. How does allowing him or her the opportunity to make the choice show dignity and make that person feel more human? How does that communicate God's love?
- Have a new family in the neighborhood over for a meal or dessert. Get to know them and let them get to know you and your family. Offer yourself as a resource for anything they may need to decipher in settling in to a new area. Doctors. Schools. Shopping. The internet is great, but a personal touch along with directions to the DMV or suggestions about the best time of day to go is a great way to show hospitality and love to new people. You can show someone hospitality just by being available and knowledgeable about local resources.

There are loads of other ways to show biblical hospitality. Think of your own ideas too. You already know that you're going to eat. How can you leverage this regular, daily activity to engage someone else in ministry? When you do that for the express purpose of helping someone, that's ordinary justice.

If you have been keeping up with a few close believers through the course of this study, consider using your regular meeting time and location to include another person this week. It's not an invitation to your meeting. It's an invitation into your life. Your goal is to know this person, love him or her, and support him or her. Your hospitality could be life changing for the other person and also for you.

INDIVIDUAL-STUDY OVERVIEW

This week's individual study examines key passages concerning the motivation behind hospitality and the ultimate aim of honoring the Lord. As with anything regarding a walk with Christ, it's not only what you do but also why and how you do it that counts. The thing about God is that He sees our hearts and examines our motives. Desiring to give Him nothing less than pure motives means starting in Scripture.

PRAY

Pray a prayer of praise to God thanking Him for the overwhelming ways He shows you His hospitality. Ask for moments and margin in life to be someone who practices daily what it means to welcome and love sick, hurt, and brokenhearted people in the world around you.

FOLLOWING JESUS INCLUDES FOLLOWING HIS PRACTICE OF HOSPITALITY— JOYOUS, AUTHENTIC, GENEROUS, COUNTER-CULTURAL, AND HOPE-FILLED HOSPITALITY.

HOSPITALITY IS A CULTURALLY APPROPRIATE WAY TO DO FAITHFUL EVANGELISM, AND A PRACTICAL WAY TO DO ORDINARY MERCY AND JUSTICE.

OPENING YOUR BIBLE

Hospitality is a thread running through the whole of Scripture. In fact, one could tell the story of Scripture through the theme of hospitality. To start your individual-study time this week, refer to your small-group discussion and explain in the space below why hospitality is not the same as entertainment or fellowship. What similarities exist? What key distinctions can be made? What is unique about hospitality?

Hospitality vs. entertainment

Hospitality vs. fellowship

It's easy to make a biblical case for God's hospitality toward us as a running theme throughout Scripture. But what about His admonition that we provide that same level of hospitality toward others?

> *33 When a foreigner lives with you in your land, you must not oppress him. 34 You must regard the foreigner who lives with you as the native-born among you. You are to love him as yourself, for you were foreigners in the land of Egypt; I am Yahweh your God.*
> LEVITICUS 19:33-34

In your own words, what are God's instructions in these verses?

According to this passage, why do you think God valued Israel's willingness to welcome strangers?

Think of a time when strangers welcomed you. How did hospitality feel coming from people you didn't know as opposed to hospitality from someone with whom you already have a relationship?

> [1]"Come, everyone who is thirsty,
> come to the waters;
> and you without money,
> come, buy, and eat!
> Come, buy wine and milk
> without money and without cost!
> [2] Why do you spend money on what is not food,
> and your wages on what does not satisfy?
> Listen carefully to Me, and eat what is good,
> and you will enjoy the choicest of foods.
> [3] Pay attention and come to Me;
> listen, so that you will live.
> I will make an everlasting covenant with you,
> the promises assured to David."
> ISAIAH 55:1-3

God's welcoming character is described beautifully here by Isaiah. What part of this passage stands out to you most? Why?

Righteous people follow the Righteous One. Beside each part of the Isaiah 55 passage, list a way you can illustrate that particular characteristic of God in your relationships and in the hospitality you seek to provide.

David is Israel's most famous king. Scripture characterizes him as a man after God's own heart (see 1 Sam. 13:14). Could a more illustrative picture be painted of what it's like to follow God well?

Read about the hospitality David displayed in 2 Samuel 9.

Why do you think David chose to honor Mephibosheth in this manner?

What observations do you have about how Mephibosheth responded to David's kindness to him?

One might always hope to respond to the hospitality of God in the same manner Mephibosheth responded to King David—with humility and respect. David was under no obligation to show that kindness. Mephibosheth had done nothing extraordinary to earn or even warrant the attention. None of us deserve the grace of God and immeasurable kindness of Jesus either. How should we respond? With humble hearts and generous hospitality of our own toward the lonely, the broken, and the needy.

In the New Testament the idea of hospitality maintains its place of value.

Read the following verses and note what each says about hospitality.

Matthew 10:9-10

Romans 12:13

Acts 12:12

1 Peter 4:9

Titus 1:7-8

Many don't see how much Jesus taught and exemplified hospitality. Jesus ate with sinners throughout His earthly ministry. He received children gladly. He taught us to invite the lowly to parties and to welcome strangers. He prepared breakfast for His wayward disciples, including Peter who had betrayed Him. He ate with the Emmaus disciples after His resurrection. Before His departure, He said He was going to "prepare a place" (John 14:2) for His people. Jesus also instituted the Lord's Supper, giving new meaning to the Passover meal, and told us that He will drink it again with us when "the kingdom of God comes" (Luke 22:18).

Based on these verses and examples of Jesus and your desire to be a righteous one like the Righteous One, compose your own simple list of ways you can show hospitality like Jesus.

As we learned in the group time, following Jesus includes following His practice of hospitality—joyous, authentic, generous, counter-cultural, and hope-filled hospitality. Jesus' command to "Come, follow me" is an invitation to follow His way of life. And that way includes opening up your home and your life to others.

OPENING YOUR HEART

Part of being a growing disciple is eventually learning how to self-feed. Paul explained in a few scenarios the difference between a mature follower and an immature one. Mature followers are ones who can handle solid food. Immature followers, not so much (see 1 Cor. 3:2). Part of the maturing process is the ability to evaluate and discern one's life and growth. The Spirit will expose our sin and weakness. Mature followers are in tune with that and ready to make spiritual course corrections along the way. One such correction might be related to the area of hospitality. A follower of Jesus who is not actively showing hospitality should ask himself or herself a very important question: "Why not?"

While there may be many answers dancing on the surface, the only one that matters is this: there is a heart issue. Hospitality is more than passing potatoes. It's opening one's heart. Because hearts are idol factories, five things must be put to death in order to extend heartfelt, justice-minded, biblically based hospitality.

DEATH NUMBER 1: PRIDE

Read Luke 14:10-11.

In your own words, write what Jesus explains in this verse.

A simple axiom for this verse might be, being humble is always better than being humiliated. Consider a time when you allowed pride to get the best of you. A moment when you considered yourself more highly than you should.

Describe this time. Who put you in your place?

Continue in your reading of Luke 14 with verses 12-14.

Jesus begins by correcting the guests at this particular gathering and now He corrects the hosts. According to Jesus, to whom should hosts be more concerned about exhibiting true hospitality? Why do you think this is significant to Jesus?

> [6] *Isn't the fast I choose:*
> *To break the chains of wickedness,*
> *to untie the ropes of the yoke,*
> *to set the oppressed free,*
> *and to tear off every yoke?*
> [7] *Is it not to share your bread with the hungry,*
> *to bring the poor and homeless into your house,*
> *to clothe the naked when you see him,*
> *and not to ignore your own flesh and blood?*
> ISAIAH 58:6-7

Pride says get the best ticket or seek the best seat. Humility says assume a place at the bottom. Pride says to invite the best and be seen with the most influential. Humility says look for the least and be seen with those most in need of influence.

A FOLLOWER OF JESUS WHO IS NOT ACTIVELY SHOWING HOSPITALITY SHOULD ASK HIMSELF OR HERSELF A VERY IMPORTANT QUESTION: "WHY NOT?"

DEATH NUMBER 2: PAYBACKS

Everything in the world operates seemingly under a theory of reciprocity. People have a problem showing hospitality without the overriding expectation of a payback. Jesus offers that the very reason to invite the poor is precisely because they can't pay you back. In reality, that's a bigger blessing (see Luke 14:14).

Believers don't care for people because of what they might receive, but because they are citizens of the kingdom of God. He calls us to love our neighbors as ourselves. We do it to show the world what our King is like, and what He has done for us. And if we have any longing for reward, we need to remember that it won't ultimately come in this life but in the next.

What if Christ expected something in return for salvation? How does Christ's free gift of salvation to us teach us about reciprocity?

To practice hospitality, you must die to reciprocity. Your guests may never say, "Thanks." They may eat all your food. They may stain your carpet. They may make you weep with grief. That's OK. You're doing this out of love for the person, because you value eternity more than this passing life, because you're simply a steward of God's provisions, and because you love the King.

Describe the last time you did something for someone else with no thought of what you might get in return.

Even the joy we get from seeing someone happy and enjoying our generosity can be part of the principle of reciprocity. In order to check your motives, practice giving freely to people you don't know and to needs you can't readily see being met. If it's a struggle for you to do this without being able to at least experience the result to a degree, then reciprocity is still running through your veins.

DEATH NUMBER 3: SENSATIONALISM

A true mission is less about sensational acts and more about simple, ordinary acts done consistently out of love. Rick Warren said, "Great opportunities may come once in a lifetime, but small opportunities surround us every day."[4]

Some might assume that hospitality is too small an opportunity, that it's a complete waste of time. List and describe some of the ways simple acts of hospitality are never a waste of time.

We cared so much for you that we were pleased to share with you not only the gospel of God but also our own lives, because you had become dear to us.
1 THESSALONIANS 2:8

Why is it important that Paul combines the gospel and hospitality in this verse?

While some may assume that evangelism is the gospel presentation apart from daily life, others assume that evangelism is daily life sans the gospel. The former may engage in street preaching or handing out tracks while the latter sit and talk about life over lunch. In truth, evangelism should be about both, presenting the gospel in the context of relationships. Hospitality provides the perfect binding agent for those two adjacent truths.

DEATH NUMBER 4: PARTIALITY

Read James 2:1-9.

What does this passage teach about favoritism?

In what ways are the rich honored in our world today? Conversely, in what ways are the poor discriminated against?

You can't eliminate partiality that you don't acknowledge or know you have. Open your heart and your head and be vulnerable for a moment. Consider if there are people you feel uncomfortable helping/loving/reaching because of preference or comfort or favoritism.

Describe your issue(s) with favoritism. Go deep to discover the root of why you think those prejudices exist in you. Don't make excuses. Simply offer authentic truth.

The first step in confronting prejudice in your life is to admit you have it. The next step is to remember some important truths.

- God's love transcends boundaries. Jesus died to save the people you discriminate against.
- Jesus loves you even though you aren't perfect and lovely. He cares for you in spite of your sin.
- Christ loves diversity. One day He'll be heralded as King by every tribe and every tongue (see Phil. 2:10-11).

You must step out of your comfort zone and cultivate diverse friendships across your prior discriminatory lines. List a few steps you would like to take in order to do that.

DEATH NUMBER 5: SELF-INDULGENCE

How do you define the word *ownership*?

How do you define the term *stewardship*?

Consider the following comparisons and circle the spot on the continuum that best describes your current state of mind.

●——●

My home is my castle.   My home is a refuge.

●——●

How much of my money   How much of God's money
should I give to God's work?   should I keep to live?

●——●

What is the least   How many people can help with
I can do for others?   the resources God has given me?

●——●

I am the king/queen of my castle.   Jesus Christ is King over all my life
                                               including my possessions.

The closer you land toward the left side of the continuums, the more dangerous the attitude of self-indulgence in your life. Self-indulgence has another name—entitlement—which says that you deserve all you have and even more. Godliness says that you are blessed to be a blessing. If Jesus is better than any comfort you have, you'll be less concerned about affording more comfort and more concerned about spending more time with Him.

OPENING YOUR DOOR

¹ We who are strong have an obligation to bear the weaknesses of those without strength, and not to please ourselves. ² Each one of us must please his neighbor for his good, to build him up.
ROMANS 15:1-2

According to Paul, people who are strong have a responsibility to those who are weak. This is certainly the premise of much of your work in this resource. A careful understanding of what the word *strong* in this context really means is helpful. The Greek word we translate as *strong* in this passage is *dunatos* and it comes with several possible meanings:[5]

- able, powerful, mighty, strong
- mighty in wealth and influence
- strong in soul
- able to bear trials with fortitude
- strong in Christian virtue
- having power for something
- mighty, excelling in something

Go back and read Romans 15:1-2 several times aloud. Each time you get to the word "strong," replace it with one of the definitions provided. For example:

> ¹ Now we who are **mighty in wealth and influence** have an obligation to
> bear the weaknesses of those without strength, and not to please ourselves.
> ² Each one of us must please his neighbor for his good, to build him up.

Continue this exercise until you have read the passage aloud with each of the seven definitions of the word *dunatos* provided.

Opening your door means that you have a door. How's that for a literal interpretation! It also means that there is something inside worth inviting someone in to see and experience. Opening your door means that you don't desire to keep it all for yourself but that sharing with others is a priority. True hospitality isn't only sharing with others who are like you, but also with others who need you.

While we should always be ready to open our doors for traveling missionaries, small-group Bible studies, and our families for extended periods of time, may we also be challenged beyond these noble practices.

The following are ideas for how you might consider opening your doors.

- FOSTER CARE: On any given day there are as many as 450,000 children in the American foster care system. Many of those are waiting to be adopted. It is not uncommon for a child to travel through five different homes and foster families. Each year thousands of children in the foster care system will turn 18 and age out of the system with a $500 check in hand to start their adult lives.
- AFTERCARE: When girls are rescued from sex trafficking, can you imagine the shame and brokenness they feel? What do they need? Aftercare ministries help girls transition out of their lives as slaves and into healthy communities.

- TRANSITIONAL ASSISTANCE: These programs assist kids who age out of foster care or children in a developing country who age out of orphanages. There are similar programs for rehabilitated prisoners and even rescued slaves. More than providing homes and jobs, education and resources are essential for people in these types of life transitions.
- HOSTING INTERNATIONALS: Some reports indicate that as many as 500,000 international students spend time in the United States. Those same reports indicate that as many as 80 percent never set foot in an American home. There are also agencies working diligently to provide education and resources for refugees who flee their countries to seek asylum in the U.S.
- THE ELDERLY: The population of adults in America 65 years of age and older is dramatically increasing. Projected growth indicates that the number of seniors in the U.S. will almost double by 2030. That means a greater emphasis must be placed on caring for older adults.
- LOCAL LAW ENFORCEMENT: This is an underserved population of civic workers. By discovering ways to encourage, host, pray for, and invest in local law enforcement, you also position yourself to be on the front lines of learning about justice-related needs in your community.

List other ideas you have considered for intentional hospitality ministry.

> TRUE HOSPITALITY ISN'T ONLY SHARING WITH OTHERS WHO ARE LIKE YOU, BUT ALSO WITH OTHERS WHO NEED YOU.

Opening your doors can be a literal opportunity for someone to come into your home, spend time with you, and even stay with you. The purpose is to meet appropriate needs and minister to them in a way that represents well the love and grace of Jesus Christ. Opening your doors can also be a very figurative opportunity signifying the intentional ways God is calling you to remove barriers, offer assistance, and open up your life to vulnerable people in your area and around the world.

Opening your doors is a symbol of Christlike hospitality when you open them up to people Christ sought hard to reach. Remember, it isn't the healthy that need a doctor but the sick.

MOVING TOWARD ACTION

As you continue your journey toward ordinary justice, this week's final segment offers you a chance to reflect on what you have already experienced. In addition to the prompts to see, hear, and actuate opportunities to show hospitality, you are also presented with the chance to express where you are currently leveraging your everyday life to offer Christlike justice in the world.

Describe how your views of justice have changed so far through the course of this Bible study.

Of what types of injustice have you become more aware?

How have your relationships and the way you see others evolved?

How has justice become part of everyday conversation in your life?

In what ways have you increased your level of prayer for vulnerable, marginalized people?

Have you grown closer to Christ through this movement? If yes, how so?

Have you experienced (seen and heard) a distinct call to speak out for any particular matter of injustice? If so, what have you learned and what steps have you taken to be obedient to that calling?

SEEING

In the section "Opening Your Door" several ideas for intentional hospitality were explained. Did anything specific jump out at you as you read about those opportunities?

Is there one particular need you would like to explore? If so, which one in particular?

HEARING

Listening to God's voice can be as quiet as a still small voice or as loud as a booming life circumstance. Consider your spiritual journey. Beyond that, consider your life story. You may have moments in your life that feel isolated and individual, as if you are the only person who can relate. More often, however, your story intersects with the stories of others in key points.

Read the list of circumstances below. Place a check beside all that you have experienced personally. This may mean you walked through the issue yourself or it happened to a family member or close friend.

____ Moving to a new city	____ Being hospitalized
____ Having a child	____ Losing a child
____ Losing a parent	____ Automobile accident
____ Going away to college	____ Losing a close friend
____ Cancer	____ Suicide
____ Abuse	____ Divorce
____ Loss of job	____ Gossip
____ Jealousy	____ Greed
____ Robbery	____ International travel
____ Language barrier	____ Family illness
____ Developmental needs	____ Other: _____

Each of these experiences should be something you listen for in the lives of others. As you hear what is happening in people's lives, there are moments when you are just the person they need to hear from in order to learn about God and receive His hand of comfort. Being an ordinary Christian means listening well and seizing moments to help carry another's burdens. You can step up because you have experienced it.

DOING

Host a party. Invite your neighbors. Specifically target people you don't know. The venue you provide to build relationships could be the start of an ongoing opportunity to minister and meet needs. When you position your home as a house of peace in your community, you're preparing for the day when someone you're doing life with will lean into you because of crisis. There are hurting people all around. Those who are lost without faith in Jesus may not know a single believer, at least not well enough to call on them in a difficult moment. But who better to speak words of life in the middle of difficulty than someone who knows the I AM!

Your party may be nothing more than family stories, fun pictures, and homemade ice cream in the backyard while the kids play together. Somehow, if you listen and pay attention, a moment to disclose your faith in Christ will present itself. You'll have an opportunity to say where you attend church and why Christianity is important. It may be nothing more than a passing piece of info. However, in that moment, you're one step closer to being able to say with sincerity, "If you ever need anything, let me know. If I can pray for you in any way or help you out with something, I am happy to help." Your guests can file that comment away so that one day, when the moment comes, they have you to comfort and love them in a Christ-honoring way.

Your party is so much more than a party. It's a strategic step toward positioning your home as a missionary outpost in your community. A place where people are loved and needs are met. A place of hospitality.

PRAYER

Pray a simple prayer this week, asking God to lead you to the right people to whom to open your heart and your door in ministry that matters.

WE CARED SO MUCH FOR YOU THAT WE WERE PLEASED TO SHARE WITH YOU NOT ONLY THE GOSPEL OF GOD BUT ALSO OUR OWN LIVES, BECAUSE YOU HAD BECOME DEAR TO US.

1 THESSALONIANS 2:8

1. Tim Chester and Steve Timmis, *Total Church: A Radical Reshaping Around Gospel and Community* (Wheaton: Crossway Books, 2008), 63.
2. Stephanie Samuel, "Ministry Is a Lonely Job, Says Pastor's Wife," *The Christian Post* [online], 2 November 2012 [cited 9 October 2014]. Available from the Internet: *www.christianpost.com.*
3. Ibid.
4. Rick Warren, *The Purpose Driven Life: What on Earth Am I Here For?* (Grand Rapids: Zondervan, 2002), 96.
5. *"Dunatos" biblestudytools.com.* [cited 10 October 2014]. Available from the Internet: *http://www.biblestudytools.com.*

CARE FOR THE VULNERABLE

HOW THE FATHER'S CHILDREN LOVE THE FATHERLESS

View video session 4 as a group and then dive into the discussion guide below.

OPEN

Take a few moments this week for each group member to share his or her best dad story—this could also be a father figure or mentor experience. If someone in your group who grew up without a father is willing to share a deeper story of how that absence has affected them at different points along their journey, carve the additional time necessary.

Use the following prompts to aid in the process:
- Best gift your dad ever gave you
- Best advice your dad ever offered
- Favorite funny story with your dad
- Favorite way to spend time with your dad growing up
- Best lesson your dad taught you

Why do you think fatherhood is so important?

Read and consider the following statistics[1]:

- Fatherhood around the globe is in crisis. In the United States alone 24 million children (one of every three kids) are living in homes without their biological fathers.
- 44 percent of children in homes without dads are living in poverty.
- Children living in homes without fathers are more likely to struggle in school, suffer from obesity, abuse alcohol and drugs, become teen parents, and even be arrested.

Do any of these statistics surprise you? Why or why not.

Do you know anyone personally who is or has experienced any of these statistical pitfalls of fatherlessness?

GROUP

DISCUSS

In your own words, what is orphan care?

What opportunities are currently present for you to care for orphans in your community? Around the world?

Do you see orphan care as part of living a life of biblical justice? Explain.

Throughout Scripture, God provides an image of Himself as Father. We come to know God better through the context of that important metaphor in our lives. Whether thoughts of God are enhanced by life with a loving earthly father or inspired by the lack thereof, God can be seen and also addressed as a Father who loves His children.

> God in His holy dwelling is
> a father of the fatherless
> and a champion of widows.
> PSALM 68:5

The God who created people in His own image (the *imago dei*) and declared them good operates in the context of fatherhood, especially for those without dads. A distinct result of the fall is the strain on the family. God's design is for children to grow up with mothers and fathers. The presence of sin in the world and the broken state in which we live means that God's design is stained. Even still, out of His grace, He offers hope to the hopeless. Through the revelation of His Word, the gift of His Son, and the power of His church, God Himself becomes a Father to fatherless children.

> Pure and undefiled religion before our God and Father is this: to look after
> orphans and widows in their distress and to keep oneself unstained by the world.
> JAMES 1:27

Name a component of spiritual growth (Bible study, prayer, etc.). Then discuss the following questions regarding it. When the discussion on one is complete, name and discuss another.

What does it accomplish?

How do you engage with it?

Why is it important?

James says caring for orphans in their affliction is one of the marks of true religion. Yet how many books on spiritual growth include James' concern? You have likely heard of and even read numerous books on Bible study, prayer, stewardship, evangelism, and parenting. If a book or spiritual growth practice draws you deeper into Scripture and closer to the person of Jesus, fantastic! But why the neglect of orphan care? Why doesn't this primary issue make it to the list of spiritual disciplines? Why isn't it known as one of the marks of an effective church? One wonders why James 1:27 isn't taken more seriously.

Practically speaking, how can orphan care become more of a core component of spiritual growth within the life of a church?

Are you exhibiting aid and care for orphans and other vulnerable people by the way you live your life? God is a Father to the fatherless. True religion involves exhibiting His care and concern for the world, particularly those who are in need and at risk.

APPLY

Do you think the problems facing orphans or fatherless children are in full view in the world today? Or do they remain largely unknown? Explain.

Is it easier for you to consider orphans across the globe than kids without dads in your own community? Why or why not?

Don't neglect this week's Action page. The way you answered the aforementioned questions will have a direct link to the action you take today and the steps you take this week as part of the individual study.

Care for the orphan is not limited to adoption. Awareness and advocacy are equally important. There are opportunities to combat the abuse, poverty, and lack of education that often lead to fatherlessness. And in this week's individual study you'll examine significant ways to do so. Remember, Scripture is not a book to be read but a truth to be applied.

Video sessions available for purchase at *lifeway.com/ordinary*
or for streaming with a subscription to *smallgroup.com*

ACTION

FOR ALL OF US, ORPHAN CARE OUGHT TO BE EXPRESSED THROUGH VERY ORDINARY MEANS.

We will continue to learn in the individual study this week the manner in which we are called to love and care for vulnerable people. Remember, it's about motive as much as method. It begins with an understanding of the biblical call of God but also extends to include an understanding of what the real needs are. Sometimes those needs are hard to identify. While orphan care awareness may seem on the rise, it's sometimes difficult to glean a true picture of global and local needs amidst other competing messages.

As a group, discuss the following:

List all the ways you consider orphans to be at a disadvantage. Be sure to think socially and economically. Consider true orphans, nationally and internationally, as well as kids who live as part of the foster care system.

In what ways do you hear about orphans or foster care in your community?

List questions you have about local and international orphans and their needs.

Now, engage each of the following discussion topics.

FOSTER CARE

List reasons someone might be reluctant to participate in foster care.

Why might believers be called to step into the foster care system?

Are there ways other than being a certified foster care provider that you could support the system?

ADOPTION

List reasons a person might be hesitant to pursue adoption.

Why might believers be called to consider and pursue adoption?

Are there ways other than becoming an adoptive parent that you could support adoption?

> ORPHAN CARE ISN'T FOR EXCEPTIONAL CHRISTIANS. IT'S FOR THE ORDINARY ONES.

For all of us, orphan care ought to be expressed through very ordinary means. While we aren't all called to become adoptive parents, we are all called to care for orphans. Orphan care isn't for exceptional Christians. It's for the ordinary ones.

Awareness is always a key issue when it comes to fatherless children and issues related to orphans, adoption, and foster care. Learn something new this week and share it with others. Start with the believers you meet with each week to walk this ordinary journey.

INDIVIDUAL-STUDY OVERVIEW

This week's individual study examines in depth tangible ways you can intersect orphans with your life. Knowing the name and story of an orphan is a good place to start. God's general will and call for every believer is that you would lovingly care for orphans and vulnerable people. Beyond that, He has a very specific call and will for your life. Is it fostering? Is it adoption? Is it supporting others who do? Is it providing resources for kids in crisis? It is most likely a unique recipe of several options, maybe something not even listed here. The first step is a biblical understanding of God's role as a Father to the fatherless. The next step is to understand the real needs. Finally, it's about taking action-oriented steps to meet those needs in a Christlike, justice-centered way.

PRAY

Pray and ask God to bring orphans and orphan care to light. Ask Him to open your eyes to global and local needs. As you close, ask God to help you see and meet needs around you.

BECAUSE JESUS DRANK THE CUP OF SUFFERING ON OUR BEHALF, WE AREN'T ORPHANS ANY LONGER.

THE CASE FOR ORPHANS

God is the "father of the fatherless" (Ps . 68:5). The Old Testament makes a strong case as to why God loves to care for orphans and other vulnerable people. Look up the following verses and answer the accompanying question.

For each of these verses, label the problem faced by those without fathers.

Job 24:9

Job 29:12

Job 22:9

Psalm 94:6

In many ways, these same problems still exist for orphans today. Children without parents have no one to speak on their behalf. They can be the subjects of abuse and exploitation. They are often poor, struggle to receive education, and become victims as well as perpetrators of crime.

For each of the following verses, note what God does in response to orphans and their needs.

Exodus 22:23

Psalm 68:5-6

Psalm 146:9

Psalm 27:10

Hosea 14:3

You could go a lifetime without first-hand knowledge of the orphan crisis. But God knows the need and hears their cry. Thankfully, churches and organizations are sounding the call like never before. Orphans need advocates, providers, and families. They need people to be the hands and feet of God's concern. And God's Word commands us to it.

For each of the following references, list what God instructs believers to do regarding orphans.

Exodus 22:22

Deuteronomy 24:17-18

Deuteronomy 26:12-13

Malachi 3:5

The Old Testament not only paints a picture of orphans and their needs along with God's concern for their well-being, but also a detailed command for believers to take on the case.

Look at this verse in James one more time:

Religion that is pure and undefiled before God, the Father, is this: to visit orphans and widows in their affliction, and to keep oneself unstained from the world.
JAMES 1:27, ESV

It's not a coincidence that God is referred to as the Father. It's in view of Almighty God, who is our Father that we obediently care for orphans. "To visit" them means to provide care. Know them. Feed them. Teach them. Welcome them. Advocate for them. Give aid to them. Adopt them.

The word *visit* is used other times in different passages to describe the merciful way in which God cares and the deliverance He provided for people (see Gen. 21:1; 50:24; Ex. 3:16; 4:31; Luke 1:68; Acts 7:23). James 1:27 is a general call. There are many ways in which to accomplish God's plan for orphan care in your life. Part of pursuing God means discerning which one is right for you.

JUST WHAT YOU LACK

There is something you lack regarding orphan care. It's something significant. Without it, you'll never be effective. It's the ability to do everything on your own. Apart from the perfect power of God made strong by your weakness, you can't help an orphan. Allowing that fact to lead to feelings of despair and hopelessness is the goal of the Evil One. For you, it would be an egregious error and ultimately, sin.

Read 2 Corinthians 12:9-10.

Why was Paul so confident in the face of his own futility?

Trust is the remedy for worry. Fear about anything you may lack when it comes to administering ordinary justice can be overcome by faith in Christ and in His ability to use you regardless of your shortcomings. Scripture is full of examples to that end. Jacob was a liar. Moses stuttered. Gideon was small. David was just a kid. Jeremiah was shy. Mary was a girl. Peter was a fisherman.

What is it you see as your weakness? What do you fear you lack?

> GOD IN HIS HOLY DWELLING IS A FATHER OF THE FATHERLESS AND A CHAMPION OF WIDOWS.
>
> **PSALM 68:5**

When it comes to caring for orphans, you probably have hesitancies. Unless you're someone who has already navigated the difficult (and sometimes expensive) road of adoption, you may be harboring irrational fear regarding the process, having never explored answers.

What do you perceive as common fears associated with adoption?

Orphan care is warfare. When you begin to minister to orphans, you'll face conflict at every level. Government is broken. Orphan care takes it toll on marriage, family, and certainly finances. It's a constant reminder of the necessity of powerful prayer in the life of the believer. It's also a passionate plea for people to acknowledge their own personal weakness. Attempting to provide care for orphans on one's own strength is futile and will cause more harm than good. Approaching the call with the attitude of insufficiency of self but completion in Christ is the only way to land. The good news for Christians is that God is for us. You can cast your insufficiencies on His total sufficiency.

Neglecting to care for the orphan isn't an option for the committed Christ follower. But how one engages that varies. Believers shouldn't land on adoption simply because it feels like the only option. Pressure from other believers or feelings of guilt can't replace divine call. Before exploring adoption, Christians should be educated in all aspects of orphan care and allow God's Spirit to lead them to a fully-informed decision.

There are three actions that should be engaged in a significant way related to orphan care.

1. ACCEPT RESPONSIBILITY.
Read Deuteronomy 24:17-20.

What are your observations from this passage?

What does God instruct people to do in their everyday lives with regard to orphans and vulnerable people?

As God offered instructions regarding harvest and normal aspects of working life, He made provisions for people in need. Believers in Jesus have a responsibility to leverage everyday opportunities to help those in need.

In fact, helping those in need should be among the most natural things we do. And it will be if we live in a constant state of remembering what God has done so generously for us. Recalling what God has done for us can provide the necessary inspiration we sometimes need to stay the course of social responsibility.

Go back to one of God's most paramount instructions:

> *4 Listen, Israel: The Lord our God, the Lord is One. 5 Love the Lord your God with all your heart, with all your soul, and with all your strength. 6 These words that I am giving you today are to be in your heart. 7 Repeat them to your children. Talk about them when you sit in your house and when you walk along the road, when you lie down and when you get up. 8 Bind them as a sign on your hand and let them be a symbol on your forehead. 9 Write them on the doorposts of your house and on your gates.*
> DEUTERONOMY 6:4-9

The audience of this address is the whole community of Israel. The opening statements of this passage are known as the *shema* in Hebrew. Shema means, "Hear!" Hear and know people of God that God is one. You are to love Him with everything. This is the statement Jesus cites as the first and greatest command (see Matt. 22:37). Then Moses instructs the people to keep God's words in their hearts and pass them to their children.

A reckless reading of this passage might assume that the last few verses are directed only at moms and dads. No, God addressed all the assembly of Israel. That included parents, grandparents, and extended family members. Some people would have certainly been parents. Others wouldn't have been. They all bore the same responsibility. These words from God aren't to specific moms and dads of specific children. They are for the entire community of faith. It means the entire community of faith bears the responsibility of passing faith on to the next generation.

The responsibility of caring for orphans belongs to the whole people of God. The responsibility of passing faith to the next generation belongs to the whole people of God.

2. ADVOCATE BOLDLY.

Orphans in the Old Testament had no voice. God reminded people to step into the gap and fill the void.

> *Much will be required of everyone who has been given much. And even more will be expected of the one who has been entrusted with more.*
> LUKE 12:48

Perhaps you are familiar with the famous Voltaire quote made even more famous by Uncle Ben to Peter Parker in *Spider-Man*: "With great power comes great responsibility."

Davion Only made the news when he asked a congregation for someone to adopt him. He attended Saint Mark Missionary Baptist Church, dressed in a dark suit and borrowed tie, and took the pulpit. His caseworker had arranged for him to speak. He spoke these heart-wrenching words, "I'll take anyone. Old or young, dad or mom, black, white, purple. I don't care. And I would be really appreciative. The best I could be." [2]

The 15-year old was born in prison and spent his entire life in foster care. After learning that his mom passed away in prison, and understanding that in three years he would be out on his own, he went looking for a family. How wonderful that Davion went to a local church in search for a family. But what if the local church was out there searching for Davion?

This story is newsworthy because it's new. Kids don't often get the chance to speak up for themselves as Davion did. Now, with more than 10,000 requests to adopt Davion, it's up to his caseworker to find the right one.

Caseworkers are vocational advocates. Christians must be volitional ones.

3. ACT WISELY AND HOLISTICALLY.

Assuming that every Christian concerned about orphans should adopt is like saying that every believer who follows Jesus should become a pastor. When it comes to faith lived in action, followers of Christ must operate with two lenses. The first is a general lens of God's will. That is the consistent plan of God for every believer to know and follow Him. Then there is the specific lens. Some people who follow God will be led to marriage and

BELIEVERS IN JESUS HAVE A RESPONSIBILITY TO LEVERAGE EVERYDAY OPPORTUNITIES TO HELP THOSE IN NEED.

parenthood. Others will not. Some will become pastors. Some lawyers. Some doctors. Some teachers. Some missionaries. Some foster care families. Some adoptive parents. Some writers. Some singers. The key word in each of these scenarios is *some*.

Read Ephesians 4:1-6,11-16.

According to these verses, what can you list about the general call of all believers?

What does this passage indicate about God's specific callings for specific believers?

For what singular purpose does Paul explain that God gave an array of diverse gifts?

Have you ever taken a spiritual gifts inventory? If so, what were your results? If you haven't take an inventory, make time this week to go to *LifeWay.com*[3] and download an easy assessment tool that will help you discover your God-given gifting. When you complete the assessment, share the results here.

Your gifts aren't always indicative of your calling, but they do influence how you exercise it and accomplish it for the glory of God. You don't have what it takes to go it alone, but with God's gifts and God's strength, you can stand in the gap for justice.

Significant ways you can stand in the gap will be explored further later in your individual study this week. It's important for you to know all of the outlets and options by which you can actively support orphans. Some will require remarkable effort and intentionality. More of them simply require the type of awareness that affords you the understanding of how to be an ordinary orphan caregiver.

ADOPTION AND BEYOND

Make a list of reasons people might want to adopt.

Would it surprise you to know that a case can be made for approaching adoption in your context today from a theological perspective? Read the following passage about a theological understanding of adoption:

> ³ *Praise the God and Father of our Lord Jesus Christ, who has blessed us in Christ with every spiritual blessing in the heavens.* ⁴ *For He chose us in Him, before the foundation of the world, to be holy and blameless in His sight. In love* ⁵ *He predestined us to be adopted through Jesus Christ for Himself, according to His favor and will,* ⁶ *to the praise of His glorious grace that He favored us with in the Beloved.*
> EPHESIANS 1:3-6

According to this writing, when did God enact His plan to adopt?

Why is the word *chose* an important word in this context?

How does *chose* translate from God's election presented in these verses to the life of an adoptive parent?

Before the universe existed, God planned to adopt us into His family. This passage was written to Gentile believers, those who had no traceable bloodline to Abraham or the tribes of Israel. Greeks were grafted into God's family not because they deserved it, but because God chose it.

> *He predestined us to be adopted through Jesus Christ for Himself, according to His favor and will.*
> EPHESIANS 1:5

⁴ When the time came to completion, God sent His Son, born of a woman, born under the law, ⁵ to redeem those under the law, so that we might receive adoption as sons. ⁶ And because you are sons, God has sent the Spirit of His Son into our hearts, crying, "Abba, Father!" ⁷ So you are no longer a slave but a son, and if a son, then an heir through God.

GALATIANS 4:4-7

What do these passage say about you?

What kind of emotions do these passages evoke?

RECALLING
WHAT GOD HAS
DONE FOR US
CAN PROVIDE
THE NECESSARY
INSPIRATION
WE SOMETIMES
NEED TO STAY
THE COURSE
OF SOCIAL
RESPONSIBILITY.

Have you ever listened to adoptive parents passionately explain the bond they feel with their child? Have you ever listened as they exclaimed that the child was every bit as much their son or daughter as if he or she had been born to them by blood? Juxtapose that with this passage. Because we are adopted into God's family, we are called sons and daughters. Because we are sons and daughters, we are also heirs.

What does it mean to you to be God's child? What benefit is there in being called a son or daughter?

A strong theological case can be made for adoption because it is what God has done for us.

Look up Ephesians 5:1 and write it here.

Next, spend a few minutes memorizing the verse. It's short so it shouldn't take too long to commit this important axiom to memory.

Have you ever encountered an adoptive family where the children look like the parents? The resemblance is so strong that you would never assume adoption. There are likely adoptive children who are told often how much they look like their father or mother. In some cases, they may disclose their adoption. In others, they might just nod or smile. Further still, with no biological link, adoptive kids will imitate their parents and take on characteristics and mannerisms simply because of the proximity with which they live life alongside their parents.

As God's adoptive son or daughter, do you spend enough time with your Father to take on His character traits? Would a stranger assume you were His direct blood heir simply by the way you look and act?

Not everyone is called to adopt and not every orphan is available for adoption. Still, because of God's mercy and His demonstration of adoptive love, we are called to care for orphans. We are all called to imitate God.

ADDRESSING ORPHANS

You may find the following categories worth pursuing as you discover how God might be enlisting you to leverage your ordinary life for orphan care.

CARE FOR THE POOR. In the developing world, poverty leads to orphans. When parents can't meet the basic needs of their children, they are forced to give them up. Investing your time and resources toward relief and development is a great way to care for orphans.

INVEST IN ORPHANAGES. Many orphans cannot be adopted. Churches and individual believers can support orphanages and orphanage workers to elevate and influence the care the orphans receive.

PROMOTE IN-COUNTRY ADOPTION. Americans adopt internationally more than every other country combined. Educating and empowering local leaders to create a culture of adoption indigenously can dramatically aid in orphan care. When political leaders use orphans as a power play, children suffer. Since the fall of the Soviet Union, Americans have adopted over 60,000 Russian orphans. There are nearly 120,000 children in Russia in need of adoption, but politics has closed the door. You can research and support initiatives that help local people adopt so that a country takes measures to correct the problem on its own.

SUPPORT ADOPTION. Many people work very hard for years to fund raise and save enough money to complete expensive adoption efforts. The emotional toll this journey takes is significant. You can financially, emotionally, and prayerfully support someone who is answering the call to adopt.

TRANSITIONAL ASSISTANCE. Children who are never adopted eventually age out of orphanages with no place to go. You and your church can build a strong relationship with an orphanage and develop a program for where kids go upon release. You can help sponsor education so that orphans are less likely to fall victim to trafficking and crime. You can sponsor education so that orphans can study and develop life skills for the work force. If you invest in an orphan now, your impact can continue when they age out.

Orphan care can seem like an insurmountable task. As you consider the role you play, read Matthew 21:18-22 to be reminded of what Jesus says about such tasks.

> *18 Early in the morning, as He was returning to the city, He was hungry. 19 Seeing a lone fig tree by the road, He went up to it and found nothing on it except leaves. And He said to it, "May no fruit ever come from you again!" At once the fig tree withered.*

> *20 When the disciples saw it, they were amazed and said, "How did the fig tree wither so quickly?"*

> *21 Jesus answered them, "I assure you: If you have faith and do not doubt, you will not only do what was done to the fig tree, but even if you tell this mountain, 'Be lifted up and thrown into the sea,' it will be done. 22 And if you believe, you will receive whatever you ask for in prayer."*

Why did Jesus curse the fig tree? In a very literal sense, the fig tree wasn't doing what the fig tree was supposed to do. It was yielding no fruit. James writes to us that it is a sin to know the good we ought to do, yet refuse to do it (see Jas. 4:17). The fact that orphan care seems like too big a mountain is in no way an excuse not to move it. In fact, it's a sin not to be involved and leverage your life to visit/aid/support orphans in their distress (see Jas. 1:27).

MOVING TOWARD ACTION

SEEING

In the section "Addressing Orphans" five opportunities were explained. Did anything specific jump out at you as you read them? If so, which ones and why?

Research will be a necessary component of your endeavor. Ways to aid won't likely knock on your door one afternoon or stand up to speak at your church like Davion Only. Your endeavor to impact orphans will require effort. Changing the course of your everyday life to include justice won't be without sacrifice. God wouldn't be honored if it were easy.

Start this week moving toward action, not by seeing the needs in front of you but by seeking out needs related to orphan care.

HEARING

We know that Jesus often retreated to be alone for times of prayer. If the Son of Man needed those moments in order to be connected to His Father, so do we.

Hear the words that Jesus prayed for you as His follower. Read them aloud so that you not only see the words but also hear them being spoken as a prayer to God.

> [21] May they all be one,
> as You, Father, are in Me and I am in You.
> May they also be one in Us,
> so the world may believe You sent Me.
> [22] I have given them the glory You have given Me.
> May they be one as We are one.
> [23] I am in them and You are in Me.
> May they be made completely one,
> so the world may know You have sent me
> and have loved them as You have loved Me.

²⁴ Father,
I desire those You have given Me
to be with Me where I am.
Then they will see My glory,
which You have given Me
because You loved Me before the world's foundation.
²⁵ Righteous Father!
The world has not known You.
However, I have known You,
and these have known that you sent Me.
²⁶ I made Your name known to them
and will make it known,
so the love You have loved Me with
may be in them and I may be in them.
JOHN 17:21-26

Jesus Christ prays that you will know God and that you will experience His glory. He prays that you will know God sent Him to love you and to bring you into their love. He prays for total unity and to be fully known.

DOING

The same Jesus who prayed this for you, as His coheir to the glories of God, desires it for the least, last, and lost of this world. Being like Christ means that you live to show the glory of God to others, too. It means you also strive for unity of purpose and vision within Christ's church. It means you desire, too, that others see and know God's love. Will you tell them? Will you show them?

Compose a list of ways you can be conscious of orphans and orphan care this week.

Now add to your list ways you would like to be intentional in your engagement of orphans and orphan care this week.

PRAYER

As you endeavor to be more aware and more intentional, continue to pray the prayer of Jesus. Pray for glory. Pray for love. Pray for unity. Pray also for mountains to move and God to be revealed to those who desperately need to know Him as their true Father.

> I MADE YOUR NAME KNOWN TO THEM AND WILL MAKE IT KNOWN, SO THE LOVE YOU HAVE LOVED ME WITH MAY BE IN THEM AND I MAY BE IN THEM.
>
> **JOHN 17:26**

1. "Statistics on the Father Absence Crisis in America," National Fatherhood Initiative [online, cited 10 October 2014]. Available from the Internet: *www.fatherhood.org*.
2. Christina NG, "Florida Orphan Davion Only Will Get a Family," *ABC News* [online], 21 October 2013 [cited 10 October 2014], Available from the Internet: *http://abcnews.go.com*.
3. "Spiritual Gifts Assessment Tools," [online, cited 10 October 2014]. Available from the Internet: *www.lifeway.com/Article/Women-Leadership-Spiritual-gifts-growth-service*.

COURAGEOUS ADVOCACY

HOW GOD'S PEOPLE SPEAK UP FOR THE VOICELESS

View video session 5 as a group and then dive into the discussion guide below.

OPEN

This week you're going to start by creating your own mission statement. A mission statement serves as a guide for the goals you set and the manner in which you meet them. It should reference your goal to follow Christ and impact the world. Write it in the space provided and be prepared to discuss it with your group. Get ready, you've only got three minutes!

Using a mobile app or kitchen timer, set three minutes on the clock.

Pen your mission statement here:

Briefly discuss the thoughts behind creating these statements.

Is there a common mission statement for every believer? Perhaps something that includes some of the following axioms.

- To follow Christ
- To know God and make Him known
- To pass faith to the next generation
- To share the gospel good news with others

The Latin phrase *missio dei,* meaning "the mission of God," refers to the work of Jesus Christ and His church in the world. Understanding the character and mission of God is a defining prerequisite for recognizing and accomplishing His plan and purpose for our lives. As displayed through Jesus, the missional nature of God can easily be described as advocacy.

GROUP

DISCUSS

How would you define the term *advocacy*?

In what ways do you think Christians should serve as advocates for others?

Who are the voiceless in our world today?

Who in your context needs an advocate? Why?

Read the Luke 4:18.

How does Jesus define His mission in this passage?

Jesus is quoting the prophet Isaiah (see 61:1) in this declaration. Continuing your read through Luke 4 reveals a shocking response to Jesus' proclamation. The people became enraged and drove Jesus from the synagogue. By promising to deliver on Old Testament messianic prophecies, Jesus was indicating that He was the one of whom Scripture foretold. Religious leaders considered this blasphemy.

The Bible provides a thread of advocacy throughout its text, calling us to become a voice for the voiceless. In Exodus, God heard the cry of His enslaved people and He responded with a rescuer. God's preferred method of salvation was a voice. As slaves in Egypt, the Israelites needed an advocate. Enter Moses. Responding to the deaths of their husbands and famine in the land, Naomi and her daughter-in-law Ruth journeyed to Bethlehem for food. There, they found Boaz who spoke up for Ruth, provided means, and prevented her from being taken advantage of.

Has there ever been a time in your life when someone spoke up for you as an advocate? What about a time when you became someone else's advocate?

Read Proverbs 31:8-9.

What types of people need an advocate according to this passage? How are you likely to view the people described in this passage?

The plea to speak up for those who can't speak for themselves in this passage is given from the perspective of royalty, specifically King Lemuel. Very little information is available about King Lemuel, but the majority of Bible scholars assume he was a king outside of Israel. Regardless of context, all rulers bear the responsibility of being a voice for the voiceless. While most of us aren't kings, royalty is easily synonymous with influence. If you have a voice, everyday justice means speaking up for those who don't.

> **In what ways do you have influence as a member of your community and even as a citizen of the United States?**

Read the 1 John 2:1-2.

As we readily engage in a life of ordinary justice, we can follow the lead of Jesus. According to this passage, we need Christ as our advocate because we are slaves to sin. He is our advocate to the Father, serving as the necessary atoning sacrifice to save us from sin's cruel effects. The word translated *advocate* in this verse is *parakletes*. It appears four other times in the New Testament, all referring to the Holy Spirit or Helper. The list of things we simply cannot do for ourselves apart from the powerful presence of God in our lives is grand. We need Christ to serve as the propitiation for our sin and the active voice of the Holy Spirit in our lives guiding us to all things true. Because we know what it's like to need an advocate, we can purpose in our lives the mission of God to be an advocate for others.

APPLY

The call to ordinary advocacy is to imitate our Heavenly Father. Be an advocate by speaking up wherever He has placed you in life.

- Social-media statuses can create awareness.
- Blogs can offer education.
- Letters to leaders in special offices can affect change.

Maybe if we all speak up, something extraordinary will happen.

This week's Action page offers a more in-depth look at how you might leverage your everyday influence to advocate change and speak out for those who have no voice. Following that, the individual-study section provides a look at key elements of advocacy and organizations with considerable strength when it comes to creating justice around the world.

Video sessions available for purchase at *lifeway.com/ordinary* or for streaming with a subscription to *smallgroup.com*

ACTION

"THE PURPOSE OF INFLUENCE IS TO SPEAK UP FOR THOSE WHO HAVE NO INFLUENCE."[1] RICK WARREN

In baking, one typically mixes all the wet ingredients together until they reach a certain level of combination. Then the dry ingredients, previously combined, are added slowly to the wet mixture while continuing to beat.

Think of advocacy as the dry ingredients. They should be added slowly and purposefully to your life. If you became the self-proclaimed spokesperson for an organization or a cause overnight, you could easily distance yourself from everyone you know. Passion can go from attractive to annoying rather quickly.

Ordinary justice isn't about adopting a program or cause and overemphasizing it. That could easily dilute other important aspects and relationships in your life. Start small and work your way up slowly, maintaining balance as you go.

Many of God's most useful advocates felt ill-equipped to do the job. Being honest, they really were ill-equipped, but that didn't prevent God from using them to accomplish His task.

In what ways do you feel unprepared to be an advocate for those with no voice? Check and discuss with your group all that apply.

_____ Lack of time
_____ Lack of energy
_____ Lack of passion
_____ Fear or insecurity
_____ Confusion about causes that matter
_____ Lack of knowledge about needs

Is there a certain people group or issue about which you already feel compelled to provide a voice? Describe the need.

How would you like to help?

This week as you connect with your smaller group of believers, talk about your plans for advocacy. Get their insight and feedback. You might even elicit their support.

Speaking up for the voiceless is part of ordinary Christian discipleship. Discipleship is not only advocacy, but it is part of being salt and light in the world. Take advantage of your privilege to speak, and take responsibility to speak wisely, compassionately, and prayerfully.

INDIVIDUAL-STUDY OVERVIEW

This week's individual study offers biblically based ideas of global and local needs that are near to the heart of God. In the business of everyday life, they would be easy to ignore. However, growing as a committed Christian in an understanding of who God is and how we have been rescued invites us to be part of that journey in the lives of others. As you engage the individual study this week, accept it as an invitation to speak up and speak out for those who cannot speak for themselves.

PRAY

Thank God for being your advocate and for offering Christ as a sacrifice for sin and also as an example of true advocacy. Ask God to reveal specific needs around you. Ask Him to fill you with a voice of influence that you can leverage to defend those needs.

> THE SPIRIT OF THE LORD IS ON ME, BECAUSE HE HAS ANOINTED ME TO PREACH GOOD NEWS TO THE POOR. HE HAS SENT ME TO PROCLAIM FREEDOM TO THE CAPTIVES AND RECOVERY OF SIGHT TO THE BLIND, TO SET FREE THE OPPRESSED.
>
> **LUKE 4:18**

WHY WE DON'T

Branch Rickey was the president and general manager of the Brooklyn Dodgers when Jackie Robinson broke racial barriers and became the famous number 42, the first African American player in the major league. In a powerful scene from the film *42*, Harrison Ford as Rickey explains why he was willing to go to the mat and endure hardship on Robinson's behalf. In college ball, the best player on Rickey's team was African American. He was eventually broken by the overwhelming racism and Rickey regretted never standing up. Rickey explains in the film that he ignored it then, but that a time had come when he could no longer do that.

Why don't believers speak up more faithfully for the racially oppressed, poor, orphan, enslaved, vulnerable, and unborn? There are many reasons ordinary Christians remain silent while injustice reigns.

- IGNORANCE: Some believers simply don't know or haven't been taught about the issues or the best ways in which to exercise their voice.
- APATHY: Some believers have grown calloused and complacent when confronted with the reality of injustice in the world. They have been lulled to sleep by the evil one, living with no sense of urgency.
- FEAR: Some believers shrink in fear of men, circumstance, consequence, and even the idea of taking responsibility and failing or being hurt in the process.
- DESPAIR: Some believers have surrendered to a complete loss of hope and a defeated attitude that screams, "Why try?" Despair differs from heartbreak, grief, or empathy. Those emotions can drive action while despair snuffs out passion.

Have you experienced any of these hindrances as a believer? If so, which ones? Describe your struggles.

Speaking up for the voiceless is part of the ordinary Christian discipleship process. We must take advantage of the privilege and take seriously the responsibility to speak wisely, compassionately, and prayerfully.

Read Matthew 5:13.

Describe in your own words this metaphor that Jesus used for believers.

Today salt is used primarily as a seasoning. Before refrigeration, salt was a preservative. It was used to keep food from rotting and becoming putrid before it could be consumed. This is the more accurate biblical image. Believers aren't simply to make life more palatable with our Christlike behavior. We're called to keep life from becoming moldy, rancid, and ultimately dangerous.

No one wants to be a useless believer. By being ignorant, apathetic, afraid, or full of despair, we render ourselves useless.

List a solution for each of these four hindrances in the life of a hesitant believer. The accompanying verses provide a biblically based clue.

Ignorance (Jas. 1:5-8)

Apathy (Rev. 2:4-5)

Fear (1 John 4:18)

Despair (Rom. 5:5)

On any given day there are tens of hundreds of persons descending on Capitol Hill for the sole purpose of speaking up for various causes. Some are professional lobbyists who represent their clients on important issues like defense appropriations, cancer-research funding, school lunches, and renewable-energy projects. Others lobby for peanut oils, equestrian healthcare, and hundreds of other causes. These people take advantages of the right to speak up. We must embrace this privilege also. And why shouldn't we? I think we can all agree that victims of injustice are far more important than peanut oil.

How can speaking up be viewed as a privilege?

How can speaking up be viewed as a responsibility?

How can refusing to speak up be viewed as disobedience?

> *Learn to do what is good.*
> *Seek justice.*
> *Correct the oppressor.*
> *Defend the rights of the fatherless.*
> *Plead the widow's cause.*
> ISAIAH 1:17

Which portion of this single verse speaks most directly to the idea of advocacy? Is there something particularly convicting for you in this verse? Explain.

At the end of the conversation regarding all the "whys" standing in your way of speaking up, only one remains. Disobedience. That's willfully choosing to ignore God's Word. It's the refusal to take advantage of biblically based solutions to each of the hindrances you experience. Ultimately, it's letting opportunities pass and disregarding the responsibility that comes with the wisdom, power, and love of Christ as believers.

PRESENTABLE NEEDS

The following is the true story of a girl named Mia. At age 12, she endured the physical trauma of being raped. The psychological damage was devastating because the perpetrator was her own father. Grief and turmoil followed. Those who should have been present to protect Mia and speak up for her remained silent. Trauma in adolescence disturbs the formation of a healthy identity. In distress, Mia sought to find a new protector and provider (enter the open arms of a boyfriend she felt she could trust). In reality, she was being lured and groomed for the purpose of prostitution. Mia was a victim of sex trafficking. The abuse she endured from her father and other men created a stumbling block to comprehending and embracing the love of her Heavenly Father. Though she has been physically liberated, Mia still struggles to accept God's redemptive love for her.

Read the story of Tamar in 2 Samuel 13:1-22.

Tamar was a woman without a voice. She was raped by her half brother. She was told to keep silent by another brother. And her father was angry but did nothing to punish the guilty. Experiences like Tamar's happen far too often all over the world. Sadly, Mia is one of countless others living in the same circumstance, broken by the same injustice.

Meet Grace. She is from Zambia. She became a widow in 2008 and was subsequently threatened by relatives who wanted to take her house. Stepchildren bullied her. They stole her belongings and threatened to kill her. Eventually, a stepson seized the house and cut off her only source of income. The International Justice Mission in Zambia stepped in with legal support. They became Grace's voice and helped her stand up to her abusive stepchildren.

Meet James. He is from Ghana. He was a child slave himself but now works to rescue children caught in the slave trade. In Ghana, parents can sell their children into slavery to work for fisherman for up to 17 hours each day. Joshua was one such child who was rescued by James. He has scars where he was hit for making so-called mistakes. Scars in his sides for not being able to dive as deep as 20 meters. Scars on his head for throwing nets the wrong direction. James speaks up for the oppressed people in his country by seeking to establish laws to protect kids. He also works to create educational opportunities for victims who have been rescued.

I ASSURE YOU: WHATEVER YOU DID FOR ONE OF THE LEAST OF THESE BROTHERS OF MINE, YOU DID FOR ME.

MATTHEW 25:40

Read Matthew 25:31-46.

Why is it important that you consider your work among the least, last, and lost vulnerable people of the world as if you are doing it for Jesus?

How can stepping up and being a voice for hurting people be part of Jesus' litany of aid that was provided by sheep and ignored by goats in this parable?

Jesus labels the people helped by sheep and ignored by goats in this parable as brothers. Why does calling them His brothers matter?

You'll encounter more of Matthew 25 and these justice-minded stories in the final section of this week's individual study.

Reflect and journal on your own hurt in life. If you have been in a circumstance like Mia or Tamar, consider what emotional needs you may still be harboring. Consider how those moments may have marked your spiritual development and affected your ability to fully rely on God. In what ways have you been stunted by the pain?

Pause now and pray using the following as a guide.

Ask for eyes like Jesus. Ask for a supernatural ability to see Christ in the world's great needs. Ask Him to expose to you ways you can leverage your everyday, ordinary life to exercise your voice for the voiceless. Ask Him to help you meet personally a Grace, Mia, Josh, or James.

COME AND SEE

The International Justice Mission website (*www.ijm.org*) offers this as a values-based statement for justice: "We don't stop at rescuing people after they have been abused. Our ultimate goal is to prevent the violence from happening in the first place." They label this a justice system transformation. The real purpose of IJM, like many non-profit organizations that work to affect real global change, is to eventually make it so the world no longer needs their work. If IJM reached its goal, we wouldn't need IJM. How amazing is that!

The advocacy page of the IJM website provides simple outlets and links where you can spread the word about trafficking, contact your congressman or congresswoman about slavery, and even sign important petitions. Since speaking up to governing authorities is a multi-layered task not always so easy to understand, there are resources to help. The International Justice Mission has released a tool specifically designed to equip you further on how to speak truth to people in positions of power called *The Advocate's Handbook: A Blueprint for Building Your Advocacy Campaign.*[2]

You might also consider hosting an awareness event in your home or community. Expose the reality of injustice to your friends and family by sharing stories and offering tangible ways people can help.

Two biblical stories come to view from this respect—the call of Matthew and Jesus and the Samaritan woman.

Read Luke 5:27-29.

Matthew (or Levi as he is called in the story) was a tax collector—the most hated members of the community. Because tax collectors were so hated, the hand of fellowship and brotherhood was withheld. Imagine being invited to dine with Jesus as a societal outcast. The collectors were not without fault. Their abuse of the Jewish populous for their own gain was a significant injustice. Although the context is certainly not identical, imagine the awareness that came from such a gathering.

Now read Luke 5:30-32.

Jesus certainly exposed the needs of sinners. He was an advocate for all unhealthy sinners in need of a good regimen of repentance.

> In what way do you think this gathering was an opportunity to speak out for forgiveness?

> If you were to host an awareness event or gathering, what injustice would be at the center of your party? Why did you pick that injustice?

Read John 4:1-30.

You might already know a great deal about this story of Jesus' encounter with a Samaritan woman at a well. At the end of the passage you see what she did in response to her conversation with Jesus.

The woman left her water jar, went into town, and told the men, "Come, see a man who told me everything I ever did! Could this be the Messiah?" (v. 29). They left the town and made their way to Him.

We know that the woman was at the well early in the evening—after the other women who had gathered water that day were gone—because of the lifestyle she lived. She was withheld a hand of community by her people because of the sin in her life. Jesus knew her shame and He advocated for her forgiveness. Ultimately, Jesus advocated for restoration between Jews and Samaritans, explaining that one day true worshippers will come together in spirit and truth (see John 4:24).

Read about the townspeople's encounter with Jesus in John 4:39-42.

In your own words, what was the outcome of Jesus' extended visit with the Samaritans (v. 41)?

Summarize verse 42. What happened to the Samaritans in the community after their encounter with Jesus?

The woman's invitation sparked a reaction from those who were invited to come and see. Hopefully any gathering you host to expose injustice and highlight needs will garnish the same level of positive response.

PREDATOR VERSUS PROTECTOR

Each one of us is a predator or a protector. By remaining silent, we might as well be predators ourselves. Doing nothing is not an option.

> *So it is a sin for the person who knows to do what is good and doesn't do it.*
> JAMES 4:17

Knowing is only half the battle. The other half is doing. Not following through is sin. Sin is punishable by death. So is being a predator or perpetrator of injustice.

Look again at the call of Matthew in Luke 5:27-31.

Have you ever had a similar response to the one the Pharisees had in this passage? If so, explain.

Let's see how the tax collectors were predators.

> *⁸ He waits in ambush near the villages;*
> *he kills the innocent in secret places.*
> *His eyes are on the lookout for the helpless;*
> *⁹ he lurks in secret like a lion in a thicket.*
> *He lurks in order to seize the afflicted;*
> *he seizes the afflicted and drags him in his net.*
> PSALM 10:8-9

This is as good a description of what the tax collectors did to their own people as any. It's also a great description of what traffickers and slave traders do today.

Jesus came to be a protector. By calling the collectors to repentance, He not only provided protection for the oppressed but forgiveness for the oppressor. Ultimately, we know that as long as evil people do evil things, vulnerable people are at risk. We're called to protect those who are vulnerable and also hope for Holy Spirit-wrought change in the lives of their predators. With God, all things are possible. It was possible for a tax collector to come to repentance. Levi and Zacchaeus (see Luke 19:1-10) stand as strong examples. It is possible for a predator today to come to forgiveness as well. In our fight against injustice, we have to remember that the greatest injustice in the world is sin and it attacks everyone. People in positions of power like slave owners and human traffickers are victims themselves.

You could make a strong argument that the Pharisees were predators as well. Jesus actually called them a "brood of vipers" (see Matt. 23:33), so the term *predator* is actually an improvement.

Jesus stood up for forgiveness that day and for the sinners who seemed outside the bounds of God's love, at least according to the Pharisees. We aren't told in Scripture if that changed the hearts of any Pharisees that day, but we do know heart change in the life of a viper was possible. Paul was a Pharisee. His heart was changed.

By speaking up, we can be protectors. By remaining silent, we sin.

Read Absalom's words to Tamar in 2 Samuel 13:20-23.

Describe how Absalom responded to his sister's crisis? What affect did this have on Tamar?

So Tamar lived as a desolate woman in the house of her brother Absalom.
2 SAMUEL 13:20

"Desolate" indicates that she never recovered. Living in her brother's house indicated that she never married. This is the final mention of Tamar in Scripture. And in two years of knowing, her brother never came to her aid. For Tamar, stab number one was the violent rape by Amnon. Stab two was Absalom ignoring the crime for two years.

Are you willing to stand up for injustice? Which of the aforementioned barriers will remain in your way? Which Tamar in your generation will remain desolate with no one to speak for her? Which Joshua will die before being rescued? Which Mia will continue to live in the turmoil of her past?

Read the encounter of Jesus and the woman caught in sin in John 8:3-11.

In what way did Jesus serve as an advocate for this woman?

Had Jesus remained silent, the woman would have been killed. She was certainly a sinner, but one could argue that the rights of women during this time left her with far less responsibility than her male counterparts. Ultimately, could she have actually refused the life she lived? We can't be sure. What we do know with certainty is that she was the only one caught in adultery that day presented to Jesus. Her male companion was conspicuously absent.

THE CALL TO
ORDINARY
ADVOCACY
IS SIMPLY TO
IMITATE YOUR
JESUS BY
SPEAKING UP
WHEREVER HE
HAS PLACED
YOU IN LIFE.
SO LET US
ADVOCATE
FOR OTHERS,
AS SERVANTS
OF THE GREAT
ADVOCATE, FOR
THE GOOD OF
THE VOICELESS.

How have you responded in the past, or currently, to sin in the lives of people you know? Do your actions compare more to the scribes and Pharisees or to Christ? Explain.

In what ways can you be an advocate for people caught and judged harshly for sin?

Jesus didn't go out looking for a woman caught in sin that day or trapped by an unjust legal system. She was brought to Him. In the middle of His teaching, she appeared. For you, the call to seek out injustice and fight for change may provide intense opportunities that you must vehemently pursue. However, the call to ordinary advocacy is simply to imitate your Jesus by speaking up wherever He has placed you in life. So let us advocate for others, as servants of the Great Advocate, for the good of the voiceless.

MOVING TOWARD ACTION

Moving toward action means accepting your own invitation to an awareness gathering. You are asking the God of this great universe to be an outspoken advocate of His call on your life to seek justice. You need God's spirit to speak and speak clearly so that you can understand and respond. Pray for clarity as you conclude your study time this week.

SEEING

You need to see Christ. It's one thing to see an image in your mind of Jesus healing a blind man. It's another to see Him on a hillside teaching. Still another to picture Him being tried, beaten, and crucified. Images like these move you to love Jesus even more, becoming increasingly more grateful for the death He endured on your behalf. Beyond that, however, you must see Jesus in the face of the victim. Read what Jesus explained in Matthew 25 about goats:

> [44] Then they too will answer, "Lord, when did we see You hungry, or thirsty, or a stranger, or without clothes, or sick, or in prison, and not help You?" [45] Then He will answer them, "I assure you: Whatever you did not do for one of the least of these, you did not do for Me either."
> MATTHEW 25:44-45

Mia. Grace. James. Joshua. In one respect or another, they are the least of these. Even Tamar, the daughter of the high king, was a vulnerable victim. When we read their stories, we see Jesus. God's precious Son was James the slave. God's Holy One was Joshua, the beaten child. Jesus was Mia, the molested girl, trafficked by those she trusted.

When we speak up for the likes of the least, we speak up for Christ. Until we see Jesus in the faces of the hurting, we won't fully understand the true power that comes from being obedient advocates.

HEARING

> My dearly loved brothers, understand this: Everyone must be quick to hear, slow to speak, and slow to anger.
> JAMES 1:19

James 1:19 reminds us that we have two ears and one mouth for a reason. Brothers and sisters in Christ are instructed to listen first and speak second, ultimately culminating in appropriately placed and displayed anger.

A listening ear is an important component of advocacy. For example, Bryant Myers says, "Poverty is the result of relationships that do not work, that are not just, that are not for life, that are not harmonious or enjoyable. Poverty is the absence of shalom in all its meanings."[3]

If we are to truly understand what needs are, we have to listen. To address only a symptom of the poverty without being willing to speak up and out for the cause might waste valuable time and energy.

Hearing begins with listening and, in this case, listening is related to research. As an important personal step toward advocacy this week, check these organizations and websites for information about important needs.

- *IJM.org* (International Justice Mission)
- *PureHope.net*
- *EndItMovement.com*
- *SamaritansPurse.org*
- *JusticeandMercy.org* (Justice and Mercy International)

DOING

Beyond their own learning, an advocate takes on the responsibility of speaking up for others. Obviously those in positions of influence are important resources for affecting positive change and distributing biblical justice. However, don't underestimate the power of just one everyday, ordinary individual like yourself. As you lean in and research global needs, God will birth something in you. Passion. Once that fire is lit, share it with others. Friends. Family. Neighbors. Coworkers. Your children. Prayer partners. Small group or Sunday school class. Your pastor.

- Forward an email
- Post a status
- Like the organization
- Retweet the factoid
- Link to the newsfeed
- Subscribe for more info (RSS feed)
- Take any and all of these steps toward being better informed

PRAYER

As you discover specific needs in your community and around the world, allow the Spirit of God to direct your passions. If you passionately pursue everything, you'll make a significant impact on nothing. Go where God leads and then invest wholeheartedly in making that cause known. Pray this week for God to intervene. Ask Him for supernatural direction and divine confidence.

Also ask Him for discernment about when, how, and in what manner to use your voice. Follow His prompting to be intentional and focused and to leverage the best opportunity to be heard. God never gives you a task, says, "Good luck," and sends you away to handle it yourself. He goes with you to empower you and encourage you. Ask Him for that prompting and equipping today.

WHEN WE SPEAK UP FOR THE LIKES OF THE LEAST, WE SPEAK UP FOR CHRIST. UNTIL WE SEE JESUS IN THE FACES OF THE HURTING, WE WON'T FULLY UNDERSTAND THE TRUE POWER THAT COMES FROM BEING OBEDIENT ADVOCATES.

1. "A Life of Purpose," *Ted Talk* [cited 10 October 2014]. Available from the Internet: *www.ted.com*.
2. "The Advocate's Handbook" [online, cited 10 October 2014]. Available from the Internet: *www.ijm.org/files/justice-campaigns/IJM-Advocates-Handbook.pdf*.
3. Bryant Myers as quoted in Brian Fikkert, *When Helping Hurts: How to Alleviate Poverty Without Hurting the Poor ... and Yourself* (Chicago: Moody Publishers, 2012), 62.

GOD-CENTERED HUMILITY

HOW AN ORDINARY CHRISTIAN WALKED WITH HIS EXTRAORDINARY GOD

View video session 6 as a group and then dive into the discussion guide below.

OPEN

Start this week's meeting with requests for prayer. Invite each participant to make note of the requests. Or recruit one participant to take notes and message them to the group.

As a group, look at the following categories for prayer requests and encourage group members to address each category.

- PERSONAL: What is something specific the group can pray for regarding your walk with Christ, upcoming opportunities, or personal challenges?
- FAMILY: What regarding your immediate and extended family is heavy on your heart and in need of prayer?
- COMMUNITY: What need in your workplace or community are you burdened about?
- WORLD: Think globally and offer a specific request about something in the world.
- JUSTICE: What aspect of social justice burdens you?

Take time to pray for the requests mentioned. If time allows, divide the group into partners or smaller groups of three or four members and asking them to pray together.

Describe your prayer life. What do your prayers typically look like?

Has the discipline of prayer truly impacted your life? If so, explain how.

In *My Utmost for His Highest* Oswald Chambers explains that "prayer does not equip us for greater works—prayer is the greater work."[1] The justice-minded believer should be a praying believer.

GROUP

DISCUSS

How would you describe the prayer life of an average believer?

On which of the categories mentioned in the Open section (personal, family, community, world, justice) do you spend the most time in prayer? Why do you think you drift in this direction in your prayer life?

Read Colossians 4:7-14.

What does Epaphras pray for in this passage? How often do you find yourself praying in this manner?

Paul tells the Colossian believers that they are always being lifted up in prayer. Paul closes his letter to the Colossian church with a detailed update about his band of brothers. Tychicus and Onesimus are faithful brothers with news to share. Aristarchus, Mark, and Justus say, "Hello." Luke and Demas send greetings as well. But Epaphras has been praying for Colossian believers. And it isn't just any prayer. The New American Standard text reads, "Always laboring earnestly for you in his prayers" (v. 12). The word "laboring" in the original Greek is *agonizomai* and literally means to "contend with adversaries, struggle, to fight."

Prayer in this sense really is work. It isn't a simple poetic formula of addressing God each night before bed. It isn't a repetitious thank you before a meal. It's the agonizing work of begging God for answers, healing, intervention, peace, and provision. This is the prayer for justice. In Colossians 4:2 Paul challenges the church, "Devote yourselves to prayer."

Does prayer ever feel like work to you? Why or why not?

Is it easy or difficult for you to maintain passion in your prayer life? Discuss.

To be a justice-minded Christian requires true humility. How would you define that humility? Discuss descriptions and definitions as a group.

Read 2 Chronicles 7:14 aloud together.

My people who are called by My name humble themselves,
pray and seek My face, and turn from their evil ways, then
I will hear from heaven, forgive their sin, and heal their land.
2 CHRONICLES 7:14

God tells His people at the dedication of Solomon's temple that people must humble themselves, pray, seek His face, and repent. Then, He will hear, forgive, and heal.

Prayer is a barometer for humility. You can't cultivate Christlike humility apart from prayer. A life marked by prayerlessness demonstrates a belief in one's own self-sufficiency. Living a prayer-free life says to God, "I've got this. I don't need Your help." Conversely, humbly approaching God's throne in an attitude and posture of prayer cries out for God's help. Before you even make a petition, the very act of praying screams, "I need You!"

> *Mankind, He has told you what is good*
> *and what it is the L*ORD *requires of you:*
> *to act justly,*
> *to love faithfulness,*
> *and to walk humbly with your God.*
> MICAH 6:8

God-centered humility and Christlike sacrifice stems from one who is walking with God daily through prayer and biblical meditation. That's the kind of person God uses to do everyday justice. Ultimately, Jesus was the perfect example of living by God's Word for the good of others and the glory of God. He humbled Himself, endured the cross, and put the love and justice of God on display. Remember that Almighty God loves to use ordinary men and women. You are a great candidate for such usefulness.

APPLY

Take a moment to describe the most humble person you know. What about his or her life indicates biblical humility to you?

As a group, commit to pray for one another this week referencing the requests you shared at the start of this session. Add one other to the list—pray for God-centered humility in the life of each group member.

This week's Action page outlines three key components of a life marked by humility. Move toward the action page with a clear goal in mind: living a humble life marked by powerful prayer and effective everyday justice.

Video sessions available for purchase at *lifeway.com/ordinary*
or for streaming with a subscription to *smallgroup.com*

ACTION

IF WE CAN BEHOLD HIM, ADMIRE HIM, ESTEEM
HIM, ENJOY HIM, BE CAPTIVATED BY HIM, THEN
WE WILL IMITATE HIM.

> LORD my God, You have done many things—
> Your wonderful works and Your plans for us;
> none can compare with You.
> If I were to report and speak of them,
> they are more than can be told.
> PSALM 40:5

The wonders, mercies, healings, blessings, and gifts of God are indeed too numerous to count. Far, far more than we could ever list or name. But it's a remarkable worship practice to try.

Take a few moments as a group to name wonders and blessings of God.
Use this as an exercise in worship.

Ordinary justice isn't about being the best version of you that you can be. It's about being the best picture of Jesus possible. The way to endeavor that in your life is to become so in love with Jesus that you naturally take on His characteristics.

Consider for a moment the humility of Jesus. It's marked not by weakness but strength. It's something you can develop.

Talk about what humility does and does not look like in the following areas:

Work/school

Marriage/parenting

Friendships/family

Missions/church

This week in the individual study, you'll dissect four ingredients of a humble life lived well—conversion, Scripture, prayer, and God's glory.

As you enter this final week of individual study, continue to pray for the members of your small group and especially the two or three friends who have accompanied you on your journey to ordinary justice. Ask the Holy Spirit to cultivate a God-centered humility in each of you, one marked by strength, one effective in change, and one easily mistaken for the humility of Christ, our ultimate example.

INDIVIDUAL-STUDY OVERVIEW

The manner in which you approach individual-study time in Bible studies such as these is an indicator of humility. Do you dive in hungry for growth, Scripture, inspiration, and life change? Doing so indicates an accurate view of you in light of God. You are someone who submits to His authority and hopes to know Him more. Or is it a disciplinary nightmare to be consistent in these moments of individual study? Could it be that you aren't quite in tune with your need of it? In either case, ask God to give you an ever-growing desire to follow Jesus and become like Him.

PRAY

Ask God to help each member create margin in life to be leveraged for the purpose of effective prayer. Ask God to birth in each member a heart like Epaphras, whose earnest prayer life produced a Colossian church fully assured of God's perfect will.

JESUS WAS THE PERFECT EXAMPLE OF LIVING BY GOD'S WORD FOR THE GOOD OF OTHERS AND THE GLORY OF GOD. HE HUMBLED HIMSELF, ENDURED THE CROSS, AND PUT THE LOVE AND JUSTICE OF GOD ON DISPLAY.

TO DO THE WORK OF JUSTICE, WE MUST BE HUMBLE AND TEACHABLE.

Welcome to the final week of individual study. The purpose of *Ordinary* is to help you infuse more Christlikeness into who you already are. That doesn't happen just by adding elements to an already busy life. It happens when you leverage the elements, relationships, and opportunities within your daily life to consider and address needs in the world. During this final week of study, you will dive deep into four characteristics of God-centered humility.

CONVERSION

Spend some time writing out your conversion story below. Pen it in a conversational style rather than using bullet points. This will help you prepare to share your story as opportunities are presented to offer a witness to God's grace. If you need help structuring your story, consider the following elements:

- The state of your life before Christ
- How you experienced God's gifts of forgiveness and salvation in Christ (include who, what, when, and where as key elements)
- The state of your life now that Christ reigns over it
- A significant challenge or hurdle you have faced as a believer and how the Spirit of God led you through it

Your Story

William Wilberforce will be remembered in history as the social reformer who pioneered 45 years toward the end of slavery in England. At a mere 5'3" tall with a chest that measured just 33 inches, Wilberforce would not make anyone's list of physically impressive world changers. It was his reliance on God that warrants him worthy of consideration and emulation. And it was his conversion that set in motion his reliance on God and his subsequent ministry.

In *Amazing Grace: William Wilberforce and the Heroic Campaign to End Slavery* Eric Metaxus wrote, "Suddenly, he saw what he was blind to before: that God was a God of justice and righteousness who would judge us for the way we treated others; that every single human being was made in God's image and therefore worthy of profound respect and kindness; that God was 'no respecter of persons' and looked upon the rich and poor equally. … For the first time in his life, Wilberforce saw the world through God's eyes."[2] Wilberforce referred to his conversion experience at age 25 as "the great change."

> *If anyone is in Christ, he is a new creation; old things have*
> *passed away, and look, new things have come.*
> COLOSSIANS 3:17

Describe what you think it means for someone to become new in Christ.

Wilberforce believed that true heart change only comes through Christ. People who don't know Jesus can do the work of offering justice, but without Christ at the center of life, the motivation will be self-centered or self-sustaining.

Some may use justice as a mark on their list of achievements hoping to earn right standing with God and a ticket to eternity. In that measure, justice as an effort becomes nothing more than an idol fueling a works-based theology. Conversion, instead, credits God's great gift of salvation offered through Christ. The change in you, wrought by the power of the Holy Spirit, isn't an effort to achieve salvation but a product of a salvation already achieved on your behalf.

With Christ at the helm of your life, your ministry of justice will be humbly centered on Jesus. God-centered humility isn't about the power you have to change the world but about the power of Christ in you to change the world.

Read the following quotes describing Wilberforce:

"If Christianity was true and meaningful, it must not only save but serve. It must bring God's compassion to the oppressed as well as oppose the oppressors."[3]

"He believed with all his heart that new affections for God were the key to new morals and lasting political reformation."[4]

Now, read the words from Philippians 1 that the apostle Paul chose to describe himself.

For me, living is Christ and dying is gain.
PHILIPPIANS 1:21

After reading how Wilberforce was remembered and how Paul said he hoped to be remembered, how do you hope that people in your life remember you?

GOD-CENTERED HUMILITY ISN'T ABOUT THE POWER YOU HAVE TO CHANGE THE WORLD BUT ABOUT THE POWER OF CHRIST IN YOU TO CHANGE THE WORLD.

Read James 4:7-10.

This passage notes the direct link between repentance and salvation. It also makes a great statement regarding humility when it comes to true repentance.

How is humility a critical part of salvation and conversion?

Read Philippians 2:12-15.

What does this passage offer regarding living a life of God-centered humility?

Continuing to work out your salvation is the idea of walking in a manner worthy of what was given to you in Christ. It isn't being saved and experiencing conversion over and over, but continuing to work out your life in light of that experience.

In what ways can reconnecting to your conversion experience help you maintain humility in your life?

How can this reconnection help you stay the course of Christlike justice ministry in your life?

SCRIPTURE

Wilberforce loved Scripture. He believed that the moral decay of his generation, which caused the very evils he sought to change, was caused by an abandoning of certain doctrines of faith. Wilberforce saw these doctrines as central, not only for the good of an individual's salvation, but also for the good of culture. He stated, "The grand radical defect in the practical system of these nominal Christians, is their forgetfulness of all the peculiar doctrines of the Religion which they profess—the corruption of human nature— the atonement of the Savior—the sanctifying influence of the Holy Spirit."[5]

One doesn't arrive at such a conclusion as Wilberforce without a distinct understanding of just how essential God's Word is for salvation and also sanctification (the process of being made holy). Humility is the gateway for understanding one's need for God's Word. Responding in humility to God is accepting an invitation to hold and protect a high view of Scripture.

Read the following verses. How does each passage communicate
what it means to have a high view of Scripture?

Psalm 119:110

Psalm 119:11

Joshua 1:9

2 Timothy 3:14-17

When you scan the canopy of God's Word, is there a particular character,
passage, or story that has remained your favorite? Why does it top your list?

In what ways has God used that character or passage to draw you closer
to Him? To keep you on the right path? To focus you on His mission?

Reading and studying Scripture is one thing. Meditating on it is another. One can't be
changed simply because of information. Transformation comes from falling more deeply in
love with God's Word. As you do, you adore God ever more and begin to share His purpose
and passion. One way to meditate on God's Word is to choose a section and concentrate
on the attributes of God described within it. Today, read and mediate on Psalm 146.

¹ Hallelujah!
My soul, praise the Lᴏʀᴅ.
² I will praise the Lᴏʀᴅ all my life;
I will sing to my God as long as I live.
³ Do not trust in nobles,
in man, who cannot save.
⁴ When his breath leaves him,
he returns to the ground;
on that day his plans die.
⁵ Happy is the one whose help is the God of Jacob,
whose hope is in the Lᴏʀᴅ his God,
⁶ the Maker of heaven and earth,
the sea and everything in them.
He remains faithful forever,
⁷ executing justice for the exploited
and giving food to the hungry.
The Lᴏʀᴅ frees prisoners.
⁸ The Lᴏʀᴅ opens the eyes of the blind.
The Lᴏʀᴅ raises up those who are oppressed.
The Lᴏʀᴅ loves the righteous.
⁹ The Lᴏʀᴅ protects foreigners
and helps the fatherless and the widow,
but He frustrates the ways of the wicked.
¹⁰ The Lᴏʀᴅ reigns forever;
Zion, your God reigns for all generations.
Hallelujah!
PSALM 146:1-10

TRANSFORMATION COMES FROM FALLING MORE DEEPLY IN LOVE WITH GOD'S WORD. AS YOU DO, YOU ADORE GOD EVER MORE AND BEGIN TO SHARE HIS PURPOSE AND PASSION.

How does this psalm describe God? List all the titles and attributes.

How does this psalm describe the optimal disposition of man?

How can having a high view of Scripture and meditating on the nature of God help one maintain an appropriate God-centered humility in life?

PRAYER

You will never cultivate humility apart from prayer. Prayerlessness indicates a belief in your own ability to manage life on your own. True humility, even courageous humility, flows from a powerful connection to God in prayer.

What is the difference between singular-focused prayer and ongoing, continual prayer?

Ultimately, you need both. Constant communion with God means walking in a prayerful attitude throughout each day. It's keeping the line of communication open and being someone who talks to and listens for God all day. However, this shouldn't replace concentrated, focused times of prayer.

Visit moments of Jesus in the following passages and describe what you learn about prayer in each.

Matthew 14:23

Mark 1:35

Luke 6:12

Luke 22:32

Which do you need to work on most—an ongoing attitude of prayer or times of focused prayer with God?

Think back over the topics we have discussed in this study. How is God leading you to pray in each area?

Neighbor love

Care for the vulnerable

Kingdom hospitality

Courageous advocacy

Times of concentrated prayer for justice-related issues are essential. These moments will continue to steer your heart toward the passion of God. If you need ideas and resources, consider the following:

- The International Justice Mission has several resources available including a prayer guide for the abolition of slavery that includes some facts on the two most common forms of slavery—forced labor and forced prostitution. You can access these through their website: *www.ijm.org/resources.*
- Pure Hope is a ministry that seeks to equip churches to pursue sexual purity and oppose sexual exploitation. They provide a variety of resources including prayer guides through their website: *www.purehope.net.*

- Exodus Cry is a prayer movement to end slavery. Download resources from their website and sign up for prayer updates at: *www.exoduscry.org.*
- The A21 Prayer Guide is an informational guide to help you pray for victims of human trafficking, for the traffickers, for governments, against root causes, for increased global awareness, for the church, and for the A21 Campaign: *www.thea21campaign.org.*
- The Salvation Army has created a resource called *Prayer Guide for the Victims of Sex Trafficking* that includes prayer requests, Scripture passages to prepare your heart and mind for prayer, and information about sex trafficking including: defining the problem, scope of the problem, demand, and impact: *http://salvationarmyusa.org.*
- The *She Is Priceless Devotional* is a five-day devotional designed to lead you through identifying with and praying for victims of sex trafficking. Each day includes a scenario, how to imagine yourself in the scenario, suggested reading, a statistic to think on that day, Scripture to study, and a prayer focus: *www.aheartforjustice.com.*
- OneLife is committed to Jesus Christ and His global mission using time, money, energy, skills, education, career, advocacy, and every resource to share Christ and serve those in spiritual and physical need. OneLife gives missions a name, a face, and a place. Their *Praying for the Exploited Prayer Guide* can be accessed at: *www.onelifematters.org.*

You might consider creating a justice-centered prayer calendar to help focus your prayers for each day of the week. Here's an example of what that might look like:

SUNDAY: Pray for your church and it's ministry to locally marginalized people.

MONDAY: Pray for orphans and fatherless children all over the world.

TUESDAY: Pray for women and children who are trafficked and live as slaves. Pray for the ministries that seek to eradicate slavery.

WEDNESDAY: Pray for opportunities to be hospitable and share Christ with your community.

THURSDAY: Pray for impoverished people all over the world who have limited access to essential resources.

FRIDAY: Pray for government and leadership in the U.S. and abroad to make decisions that offer justice to people in need.

SATURDAY: Pray for your pastor as he prepares to bring God's word to your congregation, that they would hear and respond. The closer you all are to Christ, the more His justice-minded mission will become a reality in your church.

Another option is to assemble a group that will continue to gather after this study and pray for needs around the world. Remember, prayer isn't preparation for a greater work. It *is* the greater work. Prayer is the work of justice.

> *The intense prayer of the righteous is very powerful.*
> JAMES 5:16

It's not our righteousness but the righteousness of Christ given to us in the process of sanctification. Walking with Christ is an attitude of humility. It's precisely that attitude that equates as righteousness when entering into prayer.

Close this time with a prayer offered in humility. Take a few moments to write a prayer expressing your need for Christ.

THE GLORY OF GOD

As previously stated, you can do the work of justice without a connection to Christ. An unbeliever can feel passionately about global issues. Look at the work of celebrities leading the way in social change. And look at the credit they receive. Believers can also perform powerful acts of justice and still not bring glory to God. Their acts can come from a motivation of proving themselves or earning status within Christian subcultures. But true justice from a mindset of God-centered humility focuses on one important element—the glory of God.

How would you describe the glory of God?

TRUE JUSTICE FROM A MINDSET OF GOD-CENTERED HUMILITY FOCUSES ON ONE IMPORTANT ELEMENT—THE GLORY OF GOD.

John Piper describes the glory of God in this way:

"What is it? I believe the glory of God is the going public of his infinite worth. I define the holiness of God as the infinite value of God, the infinite intrinsic worth of God. And when that goes public in creation, the heavens are telling the glory of God, and human beings are manifesting his glory, because we're created in his image, and we're trusting his promises so that we make him look gloriously trustworthy."[6]

Read Isaiah 6:3.

Often used to describe God's glory, man's sin, and also to commission missionaries, this single verse names the glory of God. He is holy. In fact, this passage labels Him holy three times. This is known as the trihagion. God's holiness declared thrice is an indication of emphasis. God is infinitely holy. Because of that, His glory is made known in all the earth.

God-centered humility offering justice to the world brings the glory back to God. Getting there is a journey. We all start with self-centeredness. Wilberforce made his next move to achievement-centeredness. Then political-centeredness. The final transition was to God-centeredness, and this is the move that birthed Christlike joy throughout his multidecade sacrificial fight against the evils of slavery.

Read the following verses and note how each instructs us regarding the glory of God.

1 Corinthians 10:31

Philippians 2:11

Colossians 3:17

John 11:40

Colossians 1:27

Focusing on the glory of God means that He alone receives credit for any successful justice-minded ministry. This kind of justice worker performs without desiring any reward in this life. They may never be thanked. And this Christ-centered justice worker may have to give up opportunities and positions in order to do it. But the sacrifice is worth it when the value on people is high and the desire for God's glory hovers above all things.

MOVING TOWARD ACTION

As a product of living in a fallen world, sin leads humans to become either passive or abusive. God told Adam that he would be tempted to dominate or be passive. The result: people, particularly men, are known for being bullies or being cowards. Injustice exists because we either abuse the weak or fail to defend the weak. Instead, we need a revival of honorable men and women who balance being tough and tender. This is a move toward Christlike humility and strength. It will require a great deal of seeing, hearing, and doing. These are essential action steps for the follower of Jesus. We must see the world as God sees it. Hear God's voice as Christ heard it. And follow the leadership of the Holy Spirit in our lives.

SEEING

You have spent several weeks being asked to see the world with different eyes. This week, stop looking at the world for a moment and take a look in the proverbial mirror. Who do you see? Is it the same person you saw six weeks ago? Is it someone more informed and more impassioned about justice? Is it someone more connected to neighbors and the surrounding community? Is it someone who can more confidently speak out regarding social issues?

> Take a few moments to journal about any changes you have experienced over the course of this study.

HEARING

For some of you, this work has likely stirred further in you a new calling—something God was already revealing. Perhaps you already felt a movement toward adoption. Your study of *Ordinary* could be God's perfectly timed affirmation of that call. Perhaps He is orchestrating something bolder in your life. Don't discount the work of the Holy Spirit in you to downsize, relocate, or even pursue a new relationship or career path for the purpose of bringing hope and justice to the world. For most of you, however, this study has opened your eyes to where you already live, work, learn, and commune. God has placed you in your current station for a reason. Hopefully this endeavor has inspired you to look, listen, and respond to what God's Word says and what God's Spirit births in you. Continue to develop your listening skills by asking God to speak and direct. Continually recommit yourself to following where He leads.

DOING

Hopefully you have already leveraged your everyday life and any additional margin you have to care for the poor, advocate for the oppressed, and show love to those in need around you. Perhaps you have found a local missions agency to serve. Begin the next phase of your ordinary justice journey by exploring the possibility of a mission trip. Find a church or an organization doing the work of evangelical justice in the world and jump aboard.

PRAYER

Have you ever heard of a camp or mission trip high? It's slang for the mountaintop metaphor experienced by Christians in moments of supreme nearness to God. It happens to high school students at summer youth camp. It happens for many adults when they spend a week or two on mission somewhere in the developing world. Seeing needs in orphanages or villages does something to draw one closer to Christ. It certainly steers one toward humility as he or she reflects on many of the things people take for granted.

> WE MUST SEE THE WORLD AS GOD SEES IT. HEAR GOD'S VOICE AS CHRIST HEARD IT. AND FOLLOW THE LEADERSHIP OF THE HOLY SPIRIT IN OUR LIVES.

The problem with those momentary highs is that they are sometimes followed by longer periods of lows moving further away from Christ, sometimes further than you were when you started. As you close this part of your ordinary justice experience, pray that any level of passion you now feel doesn't wane.

Pray that the passion is fueled even further as you develop a justice-minded heart characterized by humility. Pray that as you see and hear needs, your ability to discern and act wisely in areas of orphan care, neighborly love, and advocacy continue to thrive. Pray also that your life of justice will filter down to the next generation and also inspire others along the way. Pray for others to join you and that together, vulnerable people in the world will be freed, God will be honored, and your own community will be changed.

1. "The Key of the Greater Work" [online], 17 October 2014 [cited 10 October 2014]. Available from the Internet: *http://utmost.org*.
2. Eric Metaxus, *Amazing Grace: William Wilberforce and the Heroic Campaign to End Slavery* (New York: HarperOne, 2007).
3. Chuck Colson, *A Practical View of Christianity* (Peabody, MA: Hendrickson Publishers , 2006), xii.
4. John Piper, *The Roots of Endurance: Invincible Perseverance in the Lives of John Newton, Charles Simeon, and William Wilberforce* (Wheaton: Crossway, 2002), 119.
5. Ibid., 176.
6. John Piper, "What Is God's Glory?"[online], 6 July 2009 [cited 10 October 2014]. Available from the Internet: *http://www.desiringgod.org*.

Learn how ordinary people, doing ordinary things, can turn the world upside down.

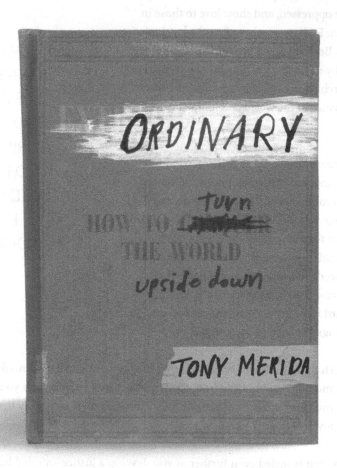

"Tony writes with simple causal clarity, radical God-centeredness and contagious missional focus. This is Christianity at its simplest and purest. This book will not only wreck you emotionally, it will change your life—it's extraordinary."

—J.D. GREEAR
Pastor, The Summit Church

Every WORD Matters®
BHPublishingGroup.com